RESENTMENT AGAINST ACHIEVEMENT

RESENTMENT AGAINST ACHIEVEMENT

Understanding the Assault Upon Ability

ROBERT SHEAFFER

Prometheus Books
Buffalo, New York

91 90 89 88   4 3 2

Library of Congress Cataloging-in-Publication Data

Sheaffer, Robert.
    Resentment against achievement.

    Bibliography: p.
    1. Success—Psychological aspects. 2. Resentment.
3. Underachievers—Psychology. 4. Jealousy.
5. Performance—Psychological aspects. 6. Social
values—Psychological aspects. I. Title.
BF 637.S8S46   1988   302.5′4   88-9987
ISBN 0-87975-447-8

Contents

1.

Resentment Against Achievement

Every society has its own set of beliefs, assumptions, and practices, which are collectively termed its *morality*. While obviously not everyone behaves morally all the time, there can be no doubt that a society's morality profoundly influences the behavior of its citizens and is largely responsible for shaping its economy, its art, its politics, and nearly everything else that makes a society distinct and recognizable.

There are two fundamentally differing foundations on which systems of morality have traditionally been based. One is the pride of achievement; the other is the resentment felt against those who achieve by those who do not. These two foundations are totally incompatible and antithetical, although neither is ever totally absent. Both resentment and achievement have existed throughout history, in all societies, although in widely varying degrees. When the morality of achievment predominates, civilizations flourish in commerce, in the arts, in science; they erect great monuments and are remembered by future times as magnificent eras. When the morality of resentment gains the upper hand, civilizations decline and eventually perish. A civilization is the sum total of all the achievements of its people, and as achievement becomes increasingly discouraged, scorned, and even persecuted, the forward momentum of a society is quickly halted, and then ultimately reversed.

As a civilization ascends, it is inevitable that its progress and growth will be nonuniform. Societies that have insisted on equality at all costs (resentment-morality explicitly made law) are not so troubled by this problem, since they never experience significant economic growth. When a civilization experiences such growth over a period of decades or centuries, those who have contributed the least develop powerful resentments as they find themselves significantly behind those who have worked, saved, risked, and prospered. These resentments are not positive or laudable in any way; if they were, the resentful would direct their energies toward raising their own productivity, and resentment would be self-limiting rather than civilization-limiting. Instead, resentment slowly brews envy and hatred of civilized society and its accomplishments. The higher a civilization rises, the more powerful is the envy it inspires in the uncivilized.

If a society, especially its upper and middle classes, strongly identifies with the morality of achievement, resentments will be seen for what they are—the complaints of undisciplined failures—and economic growth will continue. However, should identification with resentment-morality become widespread, especially within the upper classes, the resentment of the ne'er-do-wells will be perceived as a "higher morality." Achievers will begin to feel guilty for their good deeds, for achievers are people who have disciplined themselves to meet difficult goals; yet in spite of this, the people at the bottom, who have achieved nothing positive, are publicly lauded as the most worthy. Naive achievers cannot help but be confused. They have disciplined themselves to do laudable deeds, but by doing so they find themselves not in the company of the virtuous (i.e., the poor), but in the company of the sinful, the affluent. They conclude that they must therefore be doing something wicked. Achievers are thus tempted to strive for yet another goal, which is even more difficult for them: total economic incompetence, the attainment of which would presumably enable them to join the ranks of those they hear hailed as the most worthy.

Should this perversely inverted moral incentive continue to spread, the civilization will ultimately collapse, since there would be no one to carry on the difficult work of building and running a great civilization. To be an achiever is, at bottom, to identify with those who shoulder the responsibility for keeping society's machinery running and not with those who seek to draw from it a free ride. Should resentment-morality prevail, society's most capable leaders would be striving not to increase wealth and knowledge but to undo the accomplishments of previous generations. Capable leadership is not likely to be found in the much-pitied lower classes. They were not able to earn their own keep even when times were much less hard.

Achievers do not act out of a sense of guilt or obligation; they are driven onward by a sense of abundant, overflowing life. They create not merely because they desire to enjoy the fruits of their labor—which they do—but because of an inner fire urging them onward. Every hobbyist, gardener, artist, athlete, or other worker who takes any degree of pride in his or her labor is, at least in part, an achiever. In contemporary society, the achiever in his most concentrated form might typically be manifested as an entrepreneur or a successful professional, although these are certainly not the only paths to achievement, nor need the achiever possess their single-minded pursuit of a goal. Every carpenter, every teacher is an achiever, as long as that person pursues his or her work with zest and diligence. There are countless examples of achievers who, having made more than enough money to retire to a life of luxury, continue nonetheless to work as hard as ever simply because they enjoy the challenge. Every achiever makes a contribution, large or small, to the continuation and advance of civilization.

The resentful, on the other hand, are motivated almost exclusively by their envy and hatred of those who are more self-disciplined and more successful. There is no positive aspect to resentment; the resentful person has no workable plan for improving his situation, since the accomplishment of any ambitious goal requires real achievement. The resentful loathe the rich and complex civilization they see around them, which was built in spite of their surly noncompliance and their occasional attacks against those whose tireless exertions keep everything going. Civilization is the sum total of all its achievements, large and small, and the resentful feel the urge to randomly strike out at all aspects of civilization, no matter where or how they are manifested.

In youth, resentments often take the form of petty vandalism: slashing tires, breaking windows, harassing more intelligent youth, and so on. In later life, resentment may escalate into far greater violence, or it may be repressed just enough to allow the resentful person to hold down a job, although no one who is profoundly resentful will ever succeed in a job requiring any degree of self-discipline or initiative. Often these repressed resentments in marginal achievers surface as resentments against various ethnic, religious, or racial groups who have achieved a degree of success. Under the loosening effects of alcohol or other drugs, resentment frequently explodes into murderous violence, the thin veneer of civilized behavior no longer able to hold it in check. None of these negative acts benefits the resentful in any meaningful way except by making them feel "uplifted" in the only way they know, by attacking accomplishment. Resentment is success-bashing.

To the achiever, these sentiments are alien. If he does not like a situation, he sets about to improve it as best he can or to escape it if he must. The achiever is eager to help those less successful than he, acting not because he feels any guilt or obligation to do so but purely out of the enjoyment of being helpful. The achiever takes an extremely positive view of existence and is willing—even eager—to help others, which delights his sense of joyful abundance. He most emphatically does not believe that the nonachiever is morally superior; indeed, it would give him enormous pleasure to help a nonachiever become a success. Guilt is the emotion felt by those achievers who have been persuaded that resentment is morally superior to achievement, and thus that those who are chronic failures in life are more worthy than those who succeed.

Because resentment is that peculiar form of hatred felt by those who fail against those who succeed, by the unproductive against the capable, it is never acknowledged as such, for naked resentment is perceived as petty and ugly by virtually everyone. Hence, resentment must wear masks when it appears in public. It is sometimes disguised as the pursuit of "social justice," or the "class struggle," or perhaps "divine morality"—all lofty sounding terms invented to mask the ugly reality of a mob outraged by the wealth earned by others. Hence, resentment must remain a covert revengefulness, at least until it is firmly in control.

Resentment has its roots in childhood. Without exception, children feel profound resentment against their parents and other adult authorities. This is a normal aspect of childhood. All childhood and adolescent rebellion is rooted in the resentment that the (helpless) child feels against the (powerful) parent. Even if parental authority were invariably exercised with wisdom and magnanimity, which it obviously is not, this profound resentment would still exist. In this context, the preschool child who persists in refusing to eat even when hungry as long as a parent insists he eat, and the adolescent who pursues a self-destructive course only as long as it is sufficiently shocking to his parents display degrees of resentment that are utterly undiluted—and normal.

Most children are eventually able to overcome such resentments and become competent contributors to the economy of the adult world even if residual resentments may ultimately limit the scope of their future achievements. However, the lower classes of any society and their apologists elevate resentment to a moral ideal in order to rationalize their own miserable failure. As an unintended consequence of this, they become perpetually incapable of acheiving significant economic success, for to earn a decent living requires the pursuit of achievement, and the resentful are at war with achievement. To become a successful achiever, one must cooperate willingly with persons who are wiser, more productive, and often wealthier: a boss, a teacher, a mentor. But the severely resentful are far too angry to act in their own self-interest. The teacher, who seeks only to help, is seen as an oppressor; and the employer, who can be a valuable economic ally, is perceived as a powerful enemy.

Childhood is not, however, a time given over totally to resentment, for the love of achievement is also manifested extremely early in life. The drive for achievement exists well before any resentment develops and appears to be innate in every child. Watch a very small child valiantly struggling to master a difficult task, such as pouring milk into a glass, and you will see a commitment to achievement that seldom survives into adulthood. Children become angry when their parents, out of a sense of expedience, do things for them that they would rather attempt on their own; they feel their desire for achievement being thwarted, causing great distress. Watching the intense concentration of adults who excel at what they do, one cannot help but note the similarity to the intensity of such youth, suggesting that the adult achiever is simply a child whose native urge for achievement has escaped being smothered in layer upon

13

layer of resentment.

In *Human, All Too Human,* Nietzsche observes how some sick or weak people cherish wielding the one great power left to them—the power to hurt, by which they can still manipulate the behavior of others and cause the healthy to suffer the deep discomfort of pity.[1] This can be characterized as the resentment felt by the sick or the infirm against the healthy. (In his later writings, Nietzsche employs the French word *ressentiment* to designate an attitude of "impotent revengefulness." This same concept was occasionally expressed in the writings of eighteenth-century French philosophes such as Diderot.[2])

It is not difficult to find many other examples of the weak taking delight in vexing the powerful. The resentful child or adolescent adopts behavior that is deliberately perverse or shocking, thereby striking the only kind of blow against the parent for which retaliation would not be forthcoming. To take great delight in shocking or offending those who have the money or power you covet—that is the action of a resentment that is not powerful enough for a direct attack. When achievement is in power, resentment ceaselessly contrives to strike the greatest blow against it that will remain unretaliated. Resentment is continually testing the waters, gauging the reaction to its attacks. Similar behavior is frequently seen in would-be artists who, lacking any real creative talent, love to shock the upper middle class, whose wealth they envy. Also, much anti-American excess in the world today is the result of the resentment felt by poorer nations against American success and wealth; they frequently test the limits of American patience with unprovoked attacks against its citizens and their property.

14

Being a manifestation of the envy of achievement, resentment ceaselessly strikes tiny blows against civilization. Resentment tests the environment to see how far it can go. Among resentment's most frequent manifestations are petty vandalism, theft whenever the opportunity arises, the anti-intellectual disparagement of art and culture, violence and turmoil in the classroom, the harassment of achievement-oriented youth, the "rebel without a cause," militant ignorance, and the vigorous assertion of everything slovenly and ugly. Nonviolent resentment can be (and indeed should be) ignored as simply an expression of abysmally poor judgment and taste. As long as provocative and violent resentment is properly opposed—using force where necessary—it is held in check, as even the resentful expect it to be. For while the resentful envy those in power, they secretly respect them and the power they hold.

At rare intervals, however, that weak but ever-present erosive force, the blows of lower-class resentment, finds itself virtually unopposed. Typically, this is a consequence of widespread sympathy among achievers for lower-class resentment. When this happens, many educated people mistake resentments for legitimate grievances. No one is more surprised by this than the resentful themselves, who do not understand the ebb and flow of educated thought and do not expect to find the upper classes sympathetic to their grousings. They respond by striking more vigorous blows, seeking to discover the limits of the zone of free attack permitted them.

Usually, there is some limit to the forbearance of the rest of society, and violent resentment is eventually forcefully opposed. Occasionally, however, the dissolution of a society's confidence in itself and its values proceeds so far that resentment meets no effective resistance. The result is a revolution, generally accompanied by extreme domestic violence and the end of all laws to protect achievement and its fruit—private wealth. This inevitably ruins a nation's economy, leading to drastically reduced living standards for all. It also causes a dramatic decline in the degree of political and economic liberty afforded to the citizenry, as the educated tolerance, forbearance, and restraint of upper-class rule -is replaced by the arbitrary violence, envy, and xenophobia typical of uneducated people.

The glorious civilization of classical antiquity was ultimately vanquished by a religion of proletarian resentment that taught that it was harder for a rich man to enter Heaven than for a camel to pass through a needle's eye. "Galilean, Thou Hast Conquered!" the last of the pagan Roman emperors, Julian the Apostate, is perhaps apocryphally reported to have said on his deathbed. Here was a religion perfectly tailored to appeal to the lower classes; it preached that those who do well have done wrong and that those who have done nothing constructive are the most worthy of all.

We may view St. Paul as a first-century Lenin, traveling about the empire spreading resentment among domestics and slaves. "As the happiness of a *future* life is the great object of religion, we may hear without surprise or scandal that the introduction, or at least the abuse of Christianity, had some influence on the decline and fall of the Roman Empire," wrote Gibbon. "The clergy successfully preached the doctrines of patience and pusillanimity; the active virtues of society were discouraged; and the last remains of military spirit were buried in the cloister: a large portion of public and private wealth was consecrated to the specious demands of charity and devotion; and the soldiers' pay was lavished on the useless multitudes of both sexes who could only plead the merits of abstinence and chastity." Gibbon notes that the barbarians' advances were facilitated by the many young men who opted for the monastery instead of the army: "whole legions were buried in these religious sanctuaries."[3]

In the decades following the conversion of Emperor Constantine in the fourth century, the Roman Empire entered a rapid economic decline. Almost as soon as Christianity became the official religion of the empire, the once near-universal religious tolerance of enlightened paganism was replaced by conflicts—both doctrinal and physical—between the various Christian sects. Such vehement doctrinal disputes had no precedent in Roman or Greek history. Within a century, Rome itself was sacked by barbarians. St. Augustine wrote his *City of God* in response to pagan charges that it was the adoption of Christianity that led to the sack of Rome, an event which was inconceivably traumatic to the ancient world. He denied the accusation, but concluded that in any case it did not really matter what happened to the Earthly City of Rome; we should instead learn to fix our hopes on the Heavenly City of God. Such afflictions as barbarian attacks, according to Augustine, are inflicted by God upon on those who love the Earthly City too much. (When what passes for "higher morality" in a society says it doesn't matter whether that society survives or not, the society is already doomed.)

Rome's African territories, in which the "heretical" Donatist

17

sect predominated, were lost to the empire when Boniface, the Roman governor of those territories, made an alliance with Genseric, King of the Vandals, also a Christian, who was sympathetic to that faction. Boniface invited the Vandals to join him in combatting the religious persecution of Africa by Rome. He even provided ships to ferry the barbarians across Gibraltar. The Western Empire never recovered those vital territories lost in foolish battles over the interpretation of religious dogma. Deprived of African grain, Rome's economy could not sustain itself and the Western Empire crumbled not long thereafter.

The first few centuries after the Christian triumph over Roman civilization are aptly named the Dark Ages. Society's leaders sought not growth in knowledge or commerce, but instead idealized a total suppression of "desires of the flesh." The highest ideal was to be covered with filth and to live alone in the desert, unconcerned with "things of the world." The Christian victory over Greco-Roman learning and culture was celebrated in a popular chant to the Virgin: "The many-tongued rhetors have fallen silent as fishes."[4] The mighty temples and magnificent statues of the old order were pulled down by Christian mobs, and the irreplaceable manuscripts of ancient sages were lost forever in flames. "I will destroy the wisdom of the wise, and will bring to nothing the understanding of the prudent. . . . God hath chosen the foolish things of the world to confound the wise; and God hath chosen the weak things of the world to confound the things which are mighty" (1 Corinthians 1,19;27). Seldom has vulgar resentment been so directly stated. Almost two millennia later, in China, a similar surge of proletarian resentment sought to utterly obliterate a magnificent ancient civilization, again in the name of some elusive "higher ideal."

After a dismal millennium dominated by bigotry and ignorance, civilization in the Renaissance once again slowly and tentatively began to ascend. But as economic growth began to accelerate dramatically, especially with the onset of the industrial revolution, growth was necessarily unequal (for who will undertake extraordinary effort or risk if the rules state that the reward, if any, must be shared equally by all?). Consequently, resentment grew in proportion to others' wealth. Some of these resentments found conventional religious expression, although by this time many Christian sects had found ways to circumvent that religion's fundamental bias against achievement. Some sects even viewed prosperity as a blessing bestowed by God upon those who led a righteous life. That is, of course, the complete inversion of the original Christian ideal; it is a religion for those who wish to succeed.

With the Age of Enlightenment came a gradual yet inexorable decline in the degree of supernatural belief. As Western society gradually began to dare to think once again, without fear of the stake or the rack, religion began its inevitable but painfully slow decline. To be sure, many still remained content with promises of "pie in the sky," as indeed are more than a few even today. However, the promise became increasingly difficult to sell to an educated person. In an age of increasing secularism it was inevitable that someone would hit upon the winning formula—repackage the old morality of resentment in secular garb, and promise "pie on earth." This secularized version of Christian morality is now known as socialism, of which Marxism is the most concentrated form. While the two systems

19

differ greatly in their metaphysics, their morality is virtually indistinguishable. Those people at the very bottom of society, whose virtues—if any—are not readily discernible, are said to be the worthiest of all. Their problems are held to be utterly unrelated to their own individual failures; it is the fault of "the rich," who are all sinners. Both systems, Christian and socialist, stand in total opposition to the morality of achievement.

Nearly everyone in contemporary Western society is steeped in Christian teachings from the earliest days of life. Of course it is always difficult for anyone to make a break with the teachings of one's youth; this is why religious or political propaganda inculcated through early education is so effective. However, because of the dramatic rise in our knowledge of the natural world, it becomes increasingly difficult to believe the kind of supernatural explanations the churches offer, which are based upon utterly antiquated conceptions of the universe. Thus, the more we learn, the easier it becomes to question Christianity's simplistic theology and dogmas—the creation, the flood, the virgin birth, and so on—in spite of being indoctrinated in them from youth.

The problems with the moral teachings of Christianity are not so readily apparent upon casual examination, however, especially since there has been so little effective and open challenge to them. So pervasive are Christian attitudes, such as the automatic presumption of the moral worth of the poor, that we tend to overlook the obvious fact that as soon as we question the supposed divine origin of Scripture, the foundation of Christian morality becomes just as dubious as that of its theology. As a religion dies out, its residuum does not evaporate uniformly.

Those teachings that are in the most obvious conflict with reality—the transubstantiation, the resurrection, the flood—are the first to go. Thus it should not be surprising that Christian morality today remains as nearly universally accepted as Christian dogma was in ages past, even long after Christian theology has evaporated as a serious intellectual force. The decline in the acceptance of Christian morality is likely to be as gradual, slow, and difficult as was the decline in the belief in Christian theological dogmas. In many places even today moral heresy is every bit as dangerous as was theological heresy in the Middle Ages. Thus we are now in a transitional age in which Christian theology has for the most part evaporated in educated circles, while its moral teachings remain almost as pervasive as they were during the Middle Ages. Marxists and left-leaning humanists are people who have managed to jettison half of the religious baggage of their childhood.

In recent times powerful resentments have found political expression in two nominally opposing yet very similar forms. Resentments may be directed primarily against the more prosperous elements within one's own society, or else they may be directed against national or racial groups that are perceived as alien, whether they live in the same political jurisdiction or not. Political systems built upon economic resentment are broadly known as socialist. (Semi-democratic parties favoring "income redistribution" are among its most diluted forms.) Political systems based upon national, religious, or racial resentment—xenophobic systems—are broadly known as fascist. (The Nazi party and the Ku Klux Klan are among the most concentrated forms; semi-democratic parties favoring economic protectionism are among the most diluted.) Fascist resentment will typically take strong root only in a country with a fairly homogenous population where to be foreign has always meant to be suspect. To be foreign and successful in such a country is to invite disaster. Socialist resentment is more likely to flourish in countries with a highly diverse population where hatred can be more easily stirred up strictly on the resentment of economic failures against those who have disciplined themselves to succeed. Both forms of resentment may be present in a movement at the same time, although typically one form has the clear upper hand. A demagogue is one who exploits existing resentments to further his political aims.

One group of people has for centuries had the misfortune to bear the brunt of powerful resentments of both forms: the Jews. This is because not only are the Jews perceived as an alien group, since their strong religious and family ties discourage assimilation into neighboring cultures, but their powerful work ethic and emphasis upon achievement virtually guarantees prosperity, triggering powerful economic resentment as well. Thus they bear the brunt of both national/ethnic resentment and economic resentment. The fact that both socialist and fascist governments display strong anti-Semitic overtones is further evidence of the seldom-recognized underlying similarity of those resentment-based movements.

At the present time it appears that another group is rapidly becoming the focus of an ugly combination of ethnic and economic resentment: the Japanese. This resentment is especially powerful in the lower class and the lower-middle class (the strata where xenophobia is typically the strongest). Woe unto any group of people perceived as both alien and successful. (We might note that resentment appears to be almost totally absent in the Japanese culture, which may go a long way toward accounting for their success.) After the Japanese suffered a devastating military defeat by the Americans in 1945, one might have expected them to nurse sullen and resentful anger against the conqueror, as do Palestinian extremists against the Israelis or the IRA against the British, and to seek every possible opportunity to jump out from the shadows to wreak murderous vengeance. But not the Japanese. The defeat they suffered convinced them of the superiority of the victor's culture, *which they then sought to emulate.* (The resentful seek to plunder and/or kill those who succeed, but achievers seek to imitate them.) Unfortunately, the Japanese have become targets of resentment because of their high degree of integrity and accomplishment.

As a belief system of lower-class origin, Christianity displays an extreme intolerance that is characteristic of proletarian thought. Xenophobia is one of the most prominent traits of uneducated people. (This makes it much harder for them to effectively function in a large and heterogeneous economy.) Should resentment against achievement flourish, all individuality and all independence of thought would be crushed without the slightest sympathy or remorse, as happened after the triumph of Christianity. We find the same tragedy repeated in our own century by Marxism and fascism, which, being resentment-based belief systems, are likewise utterly intolerant of diversity in thought or action.

Speaking very broadly, Christianity was the movement built upon lower-class resentments against the wealth of the Roman Empire, and socialism was built upon resentment against the wealth generated by the industrial revolution. We now begin to understand why human history seems to run in cycles, some very long, others much shorter. During difficult times, all activity that results in economic growth is generally welcomed as a positive contribution to the general welfare (which it is). A period dominated by respect for achievement begins. However, as economic growth accelerates, the industrious people primarily responsible for that growth inevitably accumulate considerable private wealth. (In circumstances where people are not allowed to keep the wealth they generate, as, for example, in socialist countries, or in tribal societies, economic growth grinds to a halt.) As living conditions gradually improve, people become less concerned about day-to-day survival and become increasingly envious of the very visible wealth that some people in their midst enjoy.

Eventually economic growth reaches the point at which the accumulation of wealth in the families of achievers becomes so significant that the hatred and envy of success become stronger than the desire for continued economic growth, and a period dominated by resentment begins. Even if the standard of living is rising for all groups within society, the fact that it is rising faster for some than for others is enough to trigger profound resentment. In some societies, laws are passed confiscating wealth and redistributing income; in others the action is more direct, resulting in the mass murder of those who possess wealth. As private wealth vanishes, economic progress is halted and then reversed, leading eventually to significantly reduced living standards for everyone. When the perception is generally shared that economic growth is badly needed, resentment fades into the background, and an era of achievement can once again begin. (Unless, of course, furious resentment has seized absolute power, in which case the society plunges into a totalitarian abyss and attempting to get rich becomes a capital offense. In that event, prosperity is postponed until the repression gradually ceases, which may take centuries.)

Resentment is not to be confused with rebellion. Rebellion or some form of resistance may be healthy, provided it is carried out by rational and productive people and directed toward achieving a just and noble goal. (To plunder private property does not constitute "a just and noble goal," no matter what mask it may happen to wear.) Resentment is never justified; it is a form of visceral hatred, the rage of the unproductive contemplating the fruits of success. (Nietzsche attributes the source of socialists' ravings not to a desire for justice, but to covetousness, comparing this to the roar of a beast for "bloody pieces of meat close by" that it sees but cannot have.[5])

Rebellion may be necessary when a ruling group does not respect the rights of others or fails to display such values as honesty, fairness, and tolerance, thereby showing itself unfit to rule. However, a rebellion cannot be justified unless it is willing to treat fairly even those whom it is in rebellion against. Where resentments exist they are under no circumstances to be encouraged (unless one's goal is to undermine the society in question); the best course of action is to turn seething resentments into a plan for achieving real solutions to problems in such a way that no innocent person is victimized. Of course, one's oppressors may in some cases have to be opposed rather harshly, but if they have truly played games of oppression, they can hardly pretend to be innocents. Should a rebellion succeed, whatever excuses it may have once had for harboring resentments are utterly invalidated. If it shows any unnecessary brutality or harshness to its vanquished foes (after making reasonable allowances for the necessity of defense against attack), it shows itself to be a phenomenon of resentment rather than rebellion and thus unworthy of any support whatsoever; for the morality of the achiever emphasizes magnanimity, not vindictiveness.

To illustrate the difference between rebellion and resentment, consider the situation just before and during the French Revolution. There were many legitimate grievances. The philosophes sought to reform the government so that "the rights of man" would be respected, so that divergent views might be peacefully discussed, and so that all social classes would be equal before the law. Clearly, these philosophes of the French Enlightenment acted far more nobly than their aristocratic rulers. They did not hate the ruling class simply because of their possession of wealth and power; the philosophes had a rational plan for improving society based upon a sense of tolerance, liberty, benevolence, and fairness toward all persons.

But the proletariat cared nothing for "the rights of man." As soon as they perceived that the previously invincible ruling class had been seriously weakened and might profitably be attacked, proletarian resentment exploded into an orgy of senseless violence. Aristocrats were hung from lamp-posts in the cities, and many thousands were arbitrarily arrested and beheaded. Finally, the longing for order was so great that the populace eagerly followed the madman Napoleon, who plunged all of Europe into a series of wars that claimed millions of lives and lasted more than a decade.

The tragedy of the French Revolution was an immense setback to the cause of liberty and progress. Generations of thinkers nodded in agreement with the British conservative Edmund Burke, who in 1790 wrote sardonically in his *Reflections on the Revolution in France* that ancient Roman tyrants "were not yet instructed in the rights of men to exercise all sorts of cruelties upon each other without provocation, [and] thought it necessary to spread a sort of color over their injustice." But for the contemporary French revolutionaries, in their "improved state of the human mind, there was no such formality." He notes that even a notorious despot like King Henry VIII of England went to great lengths to devise pretexts to justify his outrages. But had he been living in the present era, says Burke, King Henry could have justified all his crimes by proclaiming them done in the name of "Philosophy, Light, Liberality, the Rights of Man." Burke used the example of France to show what was likely to happen if state-sponsored religion were disestablished and if property inherited through aristocratic descent were not protected against "the invasion of ability."[6] (I enjoy seeing complacent aristocracy struggling against "the invasion of ability": a true aristocracy would welcome such a pruning of dead wood.)

Burke's analysis, though it was cogent on many points, failed to differentiate between the laudable aims of the philosophers of the Enlightenment (many of whose goals even he supported, for Burke was actually more of a liberal than his reputation would suggest) and the smoldering resentment of the proletariat, which upon the collapse of the power of the ruling class perceived the opportunity to do what it had always secretly longed to do: murder the wealthy. Voltaire, for whom *tolerance* was paramount, would never have had anyone hanged from a lamp-post, and certainly not for some arbitrary and foolish reason. However, the philosophers of the Enlightenment made no provision for defending themselves and what they stood for against the resentment of the lower classes, which came surging forth as soon as the restraints imposed by *l'ancien régime* were loosened. This is a distressingly common mistake among liberal intellectuals; it has been repeated time and again. In their battle against the power of the upper classes, who sometimes wield it unjustly, they are oblivious to the far greater dangers posed by the seizure of power by the lower classes, who will always wield it unjustly. "Impartial justice" is a lofty ideal that has taken root only among the middle and upper classes. Over the past two centuries, the educated classes have kept repeating the mistake of judging the actions of the lower classes by the same high standards that prevail in their own circles.

From a standpoint of law, what is to be done about expressions of resentment in the lower classes? Absolutely nothing, provided that the expression takes a nonviolent form. As long as society's leaders and its achievers recognize resentment for what it is, it can do no harm, even though it will perpetuate the poverty of those who nurture it. Resentment is utterly impotent. Those whose thinking is dominated by envy and hatred of achievers will never accomplish anything on their own, except perhaps a random violence that strikes the innocent far more often than the intended victim. They cannot even start a revolution: For that they need a vanguard of capable but warped and brutal ideologues. Resentment is nothing more than a childish complaint emanating from an adult body, and such complaints amount to nothing unless those who are in a position to do something about them feel an obligation to do so—when resentment is confused with morality. It is only when achievers identify strongly with resentment that resentment has any wide-scale effect. In a healthy, ascendant society they do not.

Of course, violent resentments taking the form of vandalism, assault, and theft are not to be tolerated. Those who cannot learn to control their resentments must be locked up until they can. The severely resentful, whether in prison or not, are typically parasitic upon working people. Those who cannot control their resentments are in no position to hold a steady job. In order for someone to do even the simplest work correctly, cooperation with those who are more disciplined is required. Cooperation is only possible if the resentful set aside their anger against such people, which many of them are unwilling—or unable—to do. This explains why we have what is called the "hard-core unemployed."

What should be our goal? What is the most noble thing that an achiever can do to improve society? To help those filled by resentment to learn to achieve. How can this be done? The key element is to prevent resentment from being a profitable strategy. Achievers must stop seeking to purchase the favorable opinion of those who vilify them (a strategy which can never work, as it brings only more vilification). This tactic would force the resentful to fall back on their own capability to achieve, however meager this may be. The numbers of the resentful will continue to increase as long as the government subsidizes resentment by supporting any and all who refuse to accept the discipline of work.

And what is to be done about those individuals who are so bristling with resentment that—at least in the present stage of their lives—they steadfastly resist all efforts to assist them in learning some marketable skill? In this instance, the person of ability and taste can do nothing else but sadly sigh and look the other way.

NOTES

1. Nietzsche, *Human, All Too Human,* translated by Marion Faber (1878, reprint, University of Nebraska Press, 1984), aphorism 50.

2. For example, Diderot wrote to his family that Christianity "recruits its servants—monks and nuns—from sick spirits seething with resentment." (Quoted by Peter Gay in *The Enlightenment: The Rise of Modern Paganism* [New York: Knopf, 1966], chapter 7.) Diderot's parable (in *Philosophic Thoughts,* section 15) of the embittered man who, wishing to inflict the greatest possible vengeance on the world, retires to a cave to reflect and emerges shouting "God!" is extremely suggestive of the Nietzschean concept of *ressentiment* (and indeed may have inspired it).

3. Gibbon, *The Decline and Fall of the Roman Empire* (1776), chapters 37, 38.

4. Brown, Peter, *The World of Late Antiquity* (London: Harcourt Brace Jovanovich, 1971), p. 186. A sobering thought: We are accustomed to seeing the magnificent statues of antiquity in fragments, with arms and legs missing, heads gone, etc. I had always assumed without thinking that these were the ravages of time, earthquakes, etc., until a friend pointed out that the destruction of most of these magnificent works of art was probably quite deliberate, as angry Christian mobs savaged temples and even private homes, destroying anything that was suggestive

of "worldly" culture. Gibbon chronicles some of this destruction in chapter 28. Observe the fragments of ancient statues in museums, and you will see that in most instances, any part of a statue which could be knocked off was: an arm, a leg, a nose, a penis, a head. Here we see the consequences of proletarian resentment against the achievements of the ancient world.

5. Nietzsche, *Human, All Too Human,* aphorism 451.

6. Burke, Edmund, *Reflections on the Revolution in France* (1790), part 1, chapter 4, section 1; part 1, chapter 8, section 2.

2.
Social Classes

All societies in all ages have social classes, although there are some that pretend they don't. Invariably, societies that are seriously infected with resentment-morality must maintain, at least for public consumption, that class differences do not exist. The best example of this is the Soviet Union, which represents itself as a "classless society." In actuality the Soviets are ruled over by a party elite whose standard of living is opulent in comparison with that of the rest of the population, who must typically wait in long lines for basic necessities. Sociologists who have studied this can undoubtedly make out even finer distinctions between the two groups. For example, higher party members enjoy certain privileges that lower-echelon members do not. Urban people likewise fare far better than those who are required to live in rural areas that remain exceedingly backward.

That archpriest of resentment, Pol Pot, set out to eliminate social classes in Cambodia. He did so by systematically murdering anyone who seemed to have any education or culture, as well as anyone else who dared resist him. (Many Westerners called his Khmer Rouge forces "progressive" and called American efforts that could have prevented this mass murder "imperialism.") Eventually Pot killed somewhere between 25 and 50 percent of his country's population, until only peasants were left among the survivors. (By comparison, Hitler murdered a far smaller percentage of those under his boot.) Pol Pot actually succeeded, for a time, in reducing the number of social classes to two: the peasants and their Khmer Rouge masters. However, having destroyed his country's ability to accomplish anything at all, Cambodia was attacked and easily overrun by its Communist neighbor Vietnam, whose own assault upon its citizens of ability was less ferocious. (Those who say that war is caused by capitalist greed have never explained the 1979 war between Communist Cambodia and Communist Vietnam.)

In *The Genealogy of Morals,* Nietzsche observes that the etymological derivation of terms for "good" in various languages traces back to the words for "aristocratic" or "noble." Similarly, terms meaning "plebian" or "vulgar" evolve finally into "bad." The ancient Greek aristocracy referred to themselves as "we truthful ones," which placed outside the pale the lying or vulgar man. Nietzsche describes the ancient "aristocratic equation" of morality, the concept prevailing throughout the pagan period of classical antiquity, as "good = aristocratic = beautiful = happy

= loved by the gods." He contrasts this with the moral equation established by Christianity, which prevails even today: "The wretched alone are the good; the poor, the weak, the lowly, are alone the good."[1] This is obviously the complete inversion of the original idea; such a scheme must clearly have been devised by the lower classes to attempt to cast an aura of sanctity over their wretchedness. It is probably not a coincidence that learning and civilization collapsed not long after this view became widespread. Nietzsche undertook what he called "the re-valuation of all values" in an attempt to combat Christian and socialist morality and pave the way for what he hoped would be a resurgence of the Hellenic spirit.

Nietzsche makes the same point in *Beyond Good and Evil,* observing that "it is a fundamental belief of all aristocrats that the common people are untruthful."[2] He suggests that if the aristocratic elements in society—"we truthful ones" to the Greeks—do not cause their own moral values to prevail, then the "slave morality" of the presumably mendacious lower classes will. The facts suggest that this analysis contains considerable elements of truth, elements that are seldom recognized. Nietzsche's analysis would predict that a proletarian state, should one come into existence, would be the most mendacious in all history. Since the time of Nietzsche, one has, and it is. This concept also explains why the crime rate is astronomically high in proletarian areas of major cities, yet extremely low in affluent suburban areas. The values of many among the lower classes tolerate and even encourage the theft, cheating, and scams of every description that are prevalent in the areas they inhabit. The noble values of honesty, respect for persons and property, and fairness prevail in the realms of the affluent because in the absence of such values one cannot generate wealth. In a capitalist, free society, wealth is the consequence of a lifetime of commitments honored.

Most people think that *aristocracy* means "rule by a hereditary elite." But it does not. It is derived from the Greek word *aristos,* meaning "the best." *Aristocracy* literally means "rule by the best," a concept which in the abstract is difficult to argue against even if in practice it often does not work out as its proponents intend. Aristotle was careful to distinguish between *aristocracy*—the generous and magnanimous rule of the best, which he held to be desirable—and *oligarchy,* the rule by an unscrupulous few seeking self-advancement. Modern people, who seldom read ancient texts, tend to confuse the latter with the former. *Plutocracy* is literally the rule by "the wealthy."

Even Thomas Jefferson expected that there would be a "natural aristocracy" in America, although not necessarily a hereditary one. "May we not even say," wrote Jefferson to John Adams in 1813, that "that form of government is best which provides the most effectually for a pure selection of these natural *aristoi* into the offices of government? The artificial aristocracy is a mischevious ingredient in government, and provision should be made to prevent its ascendancy. . . . I think the best remedy is exactly that provided by all our constitutions, to leave to the citizens the free election and separation of the aristoi from the *pseudo-aristoi,* of the wheat from the chaff. In general they will elect the really good and wise. In some instances, wealth may corrupt, and birth blind them; but not in sufficient degree to endanger the society."[3] What socialism seeks to establish is

36

a *kakos-ocracy*—"the rule by the worst" (a noneuphonious term for a form of government which seems not to have occurred to the ancient Greeks)—i.e., government by those elements that seek to rule precisely because they have failed in open economic competition.

Some believe that low-income people steal what they need because they are poor. But the reverse is true: many of these people are poor because they think that wealth is best acquired through theft. To generate any appreciable degree of long-term affluence requires scrupulous honesty and the willingness to honor long-term agreements with employers, suppliers, partners, and especially customers. The flimflam artist may generate a few quick bucks through fraud or misrepresentation, but no successful and lasting business enterprise was ever founded on such principles. Not only must a business cultivate repeat customers in order to be successful, but it must avoid losing lawsuits as well; and given juries' propensities for making lavish judgments against major corporations whom they find guilty of wrongdoing, honesty becomes the only business policy that will work in the long term. The modern-day proletarian who relishes hustles and scams forges a powerful chain binding him to his poverty.

Furthermore, if poor people were indeed stealing to meet their daily needs, there would be more stealing of staple items like food and clothing—not luxury items like stereos, cameras, jewelry, automobiles and automobile parts, and so on, which make up the bulk of the loot. But since the cost of basic necessities is entirely covered by various welfare programs, these people are clearly not stealing to stay alive. Most of the stolen items are fenced for money to finance things like drugs, gambling, and fancy cars. (The ghost of *Les Miserables* remains with us long after it should have been exorcised by common sense. An interesting question is, why did Ayn Rand, who in other matters displayed such concise thinking, praise to the skies only the novels of Victor Hugo, which depict the "virtuous" poor being exploited by a cruel society?)

In a socialist or tribal society, some of the poor may indeed be virtuous, since to be competent and hard-working in such a society comes to naught; the fruit of achievement is automatically confiscated. Similarly, in backward rural environments, some people may work very hard yet still fail to get very far ahead, their poor productivity owing primarily to the overall lack of capital investment in their local economy. In any complex economic environment approximating free-market capitalism, unskilled but hard-working immigrants who enter penniless can blend in to the middle class within a few short years. But to be born into such a society and remain poor year after year amounts to a public declaration of economic incompetence.

Further evidence against the commonly held notion that the poor are reluctantly "forced" into crime by "economic exploitation" is the gratuitous vandalism and violence that frequently accompany such crime. Victims of lower-class crime are very often cruelly beaten, stabbed, or shot, even when not resisting in any way. Sadly, many among the lower classes seem to enjoy this criminal violence very much (males brag about such acts of brutality during their displays of proletarian machismo); and the cult of violence permeates much of rock music—the musical expression of slum values. The source of this unnecessary and inhuman violence is the proletarian criminal's seething resentment against those who have disciplined themselves to succeed in areas where he has failed. However, for the duration of a robbery or other crime, a productive, law-abiding citizen is wholly at the mercy of one who is violently resentful. The gratuitous injury and violence is the criminal's way of releasing a lifetime of seething anger against successful people such as these, one of whom he now holds completely under his power. In her book *Totalitarianism,* Hannah Arendt notes that a great deal of the inhuman torture inflicted needlessly upon concentration camp inmates by the "criminal and abnormal" elements of Hitler's special SA force was permitted as a reward "for services rendered" to the regime. "Behind the blind bestiality of the SA, there often lay a deep hatred and resentment of all those who were socially, intellectually, or physically better off than themselves, and who now, as if in fulfillment of their wildest dreams, were in their power."[4]

Nietzsche suggests that morality as a concept is derived from power and strength, and hence can exist only between peers. However, this would seem to contradict his idea of the higher man being exceedingly truthful, being capable of binding himself by his promises.[5] The requirement that a higher man be truthful implies that he must be truthful even to those below him, both for logical consistency and for practical reasons as well. If I fail to keep an agreement with my gardener or butler, does not that make me as mendacious as the worst proletarian offenders? And does it not thus place me outside "we truthful ones"? As a practical matter, simple economic cooperation between persons of high and low status (which must occur in all societies) imposes on everyone the obligation to be truthful in such dealings, or the entire edifice collapses.

Clearly the noble man cannot be the first to defect, for that is the indisputable province of the proletarian. In recent decades mathematicians have devised the concept of *games theory* to describe the results of playing out certain strategies as two or more parties interact with each other, each seeking their own best advantage. Consider the possible strategies for economic transactions: "I always keep my word, even if the other party cheats me"; "I always cheat first"; "I never cheat unless the other party cheats me first." Computer simulations of economic interactions based on these strategies were carried out by Robert Axelrod, and described in *The Evolution of Economic Cooperation,* a book which examines the possible origins of "spontaneous economic order." The strategy "I always cheat" works only in the scenario in which the players never encounter each other again. The most successful strategy of all over the long term, in a society where individuals encounter each other repeatedly, is the one called *tit-for-tat:* "I cooperate with the other party, unless and until he cheats me. If he does, I retaliate, then afterwards forgive him and am prepared to cooperate again." *Tit-for-tat* won hands-down against every other strategy and was far more successful than those based on exploitation or deception of the other party.[6]

Thus the emergence of a group pursuing self-advancement through honest behavior on top of every developed society is not due to "exploitation of the masses" or to some bizarre co-incidence; it is a predictable consequence of mathematical laws. Similarly, the proletarian's economic failure is not due to a sinister conspiracy or to prejudice against him, but is an inevitable consequence of his fondness for mendacity; he is playing by a script that is a certain loser. Surprisingly, Axelrod found that a group practicing defection (i.e., mendacity) can in some circumstances be successfully "invaded" and bested by a cluster of people as small as 5 percent of the total practicing *tit-for-tat,* which at first trades primarily among itself, then gradually expands outward. This suggests that aristocracies, at least in relatively developed commercial societies, may not have achieved their position through conquest in war, as is generally supposed; they may have gained their advantageous position by starting out as that original small minority that was truthful enough to practice a winning economic strategy.

Consider that sense of fair play the British upper classes possess to a remarkable degree. Even when dealing with a determined adversary, their noble outlook insists that one must not take unfair advantage of one's own position of strength. It makes one unfailingly self-policing. In such circles a person would be perceived as unworthy of his station were he to fail to treat a stranger, a competitor, or even an opponent fairly, or to fail to give such a person the benefit of every possible doubt. He would not be among "we truthful ones." In debates in the British House of Lords, the peers are expected to be ceaselessly self-policing. It is considered unacceptable for anyone to advocate any position from which he might personally stand to gain without first clearly disclosing that fact. Consequently the Lords are forever saying things like, "Before proceeding further I think I should declare an interest," or "Before I begin, perhaps I should say that I have an interest in it," lest anyone assume that they might be trying to benefit through deceitful concealment.

41

SOCIAL CLASSES

These are the noble values, although one need not be born an aristocrat to hold or share them. Today the bourgeoisie, especially the haute-bourgeoisie, share this outlook to a considerable degree. There are no old-line aristocrats actually running a major government today anywhere in the world; they have all ceded their powers to the bourgeoisie, in most instances without a fight. After all, isn't it only fair that the people should have the final word on how they should be governed? Today's bourgeois states are the legitimate successors of the aristocratic regimes of a century or two earlier. Even the notoriously autocratic and uncompromising Czar of Russia eventually resigned graciously when he saw that he had to, and ceded power to a bourgeois coalition, which unfortunately was unable to retain it.

Today the noble morality that once characterized the aristocracy—that emphasis on truth, fair play, and a respect for others' rights—has expanded to encompass most of the bourgeoisie. Put simply, many upper-class values have successfully diffused downward. It is only in this context of honesty as the norm that capital investment, which generates affluence, becomes possible; for when savings are routinely plundered, all attempts to save come to an end. It is only in such a context of truthfulness that a pluralistic society, emphasizing respect for and tolerance of others' opinions, property, and way of life, can exist. We who live in the Western democracies can justifiably take pride in the large percentage of our population that is made up of, for the most part, "truthful ones."

Some will object to this analysis by pointing to certain widely publicized instances of dishonest behavior among the wealthy. That one can cite a few instances of this kind does not invalidate

ROBERT SHEAFFER

the analysis, any more than does the fact that one can point
to a few instances of great self-disinterested truthfulness among
the proletariat. Indeed, that instances like these make headlines
suggests how rare they really are. Speaking of norms, consider,
for example, the great truthfulness required to become a successful
banker, who handles huge sums of other peoples' money every
day. No one will deposit even one cent in any bank unless
convinced of the utter trustworthiness of the person setting up
and managing the account. The fact that people worry far more
about the bank failing through unwise investment than about
the banker absconding with the funds shows that everyone
subconsciously realizes that far higher standards of honesty prevail
in large banks than out in the street. Every banker must bend
over backward to reassure depositors that their money will be
available whenever they need it, for a bank literally has nothing
if it does not have a reputation for scrupulous honesty. Many
people enjoy repeating the popular notion that the wealthy are
cheating vultures, while the poor are virtuous and honest. Yet
anyone who doubts that the ethics prevailing among wealthy
bankers and stockbrokers are vastly more honest than those of
slum dwellers should avoid all financial institutions like the plague.

Now contrast the scrupulous honesty prevailing in financial
circles with the ethics and morals that are common in the lower
classes. Theft, violence, vandalism, and fraud run rampant in
slum areas in every major Western city, and this is considered
absolutely normal by many who live there. A walk through such
areas involves the serious risk of being assaulted, especially at
night. If the electric power goes off for a few hours across a
major city, rendering burglar alarms ineffective and hampering

43

normal surveillance by law enforcement officers, hordes of savages surge out of proletarian areas and loot any unfortunate merchant whose inventory is within reach.

Those who are particularly vulnerable—the elderly, the frail, the young—are singled out as easy targets. Gangs of delinquents prey upon the elderly or the infirm, frequently inflicting cruel and unnecessary injury in addition to plundering valuables. This is the complete negation of every noble, civilized value, which seeks to protect the helpless as well as the strong. It emphasizes plunder, not production. Confidence schemes and scams of every description abound. Far from being censured, those who obtain money through theft, extortion, or fraud are held in high esteem among many slum-dwellers, and become role models for youth. Such are proletarian values, and they are the same whether exercised singly, by a lone thief, or collectively, following the seizure of state power by the proletariat.

This dismal scenario is not limited to any one country or region. The writings of anthropologist Oscar Lewis provide a clear illustration of proletarian thinking and the proletarian way of life by simply allowing these people to tell their life stories in their own words. In *The Children of Sanchez,* we read about life in a Mexican slum. In *La Vida* it is the life history of a Puerto Rican family which moves to a New York City slum.[7] In each case the story is much the same: alcoholism, domestic violence, constant quarreling, theft, arbitrary and senseless brutality, the flight from responsibility, and the repeated failure to do anything whatsoever to remedy the situation. It is pointless to ask why such people are poor; given the values they exhibit, it could be no other way.

ROBERT SHEAFFER

The so-called "class struggle" is nothing but the ongoing assault of resentment against achievement. Today, when we hear the term "class struggle," we think exclusively of Marxism-Leninism, its most contemporary manifestation. We forget that Christianity itself is very much a part of the "class struggle," which is the ceaseless attack of angry failure against visible success. In fact, class hatred was the impetus that got Christianity going. It preaches that the undisciplined and the stupid, "enlightened" by dubious mystical doctrines and bolstered by questionable "miracles," are incomparably more worthy than all the learned sages of Greece and Rome, who had already laid down foundations of philosophy, mathematics, and astronomy (glorious achievements which are still celebrated to this day). Christianity, with its hostility toward worldly success and its promotion of suffering and guilt, succeeded in reversing economic growth and stifling learning for a full millennium. Even today, Christian values hold millions of individuals and even entire countries in dismal poverty as they attempt to honor the dictate "Blessed are the Poor," and sacrifice success in the life they have now for the illusion of happiness in a promised life to follow.

An emphasis on self-development and achievement characterizes the aristocratic/haut-bourgeois outlook, wherein the noble values of justice, honesty, tolerance of differences, and fair play for everyone are esteemed as the highest ideals. Individual responsibility is a cornerstone of this outlook; achievers not only expect and fully intend to pay their own way, but they support their own dependent families, contribute to the support of causes deemed worthy, and nonetheless manage to support the non-working poor through taxation. Anyone who fails to live up to such ideals in professional or managerial circles is harshly judged. Not only do achievers fully expect to pay their own bills, but they are resigned to the idea that they will contribute to the support of numerous hangers-on who can not or will not support themselves.

On the other hand, the proletarian outlook is dominated by resentment, which is frequently expressed through arbitrary and senseless violence, theft, plunder, and vandalism. The resentful feel no obligation to support themselves. They know that some soft-hearted person who will be moved by their self-made plight can always be found. The resentful do not respect the persons or properties of others; purses are made to be snatched, cars are made to be stolen, and windows are made to be smashed. The morality of achievement is utterly foreign to them. Anyone who tries to "make it in the system" is a patsy, a fool, or has been taken in by ruling-class propaganda. The prime role models for success for many slum-dwellers are the clever thief, the drug dealer, the pimp.

Of course, not all persons residing in proletarian areas share these miserable values; such persons are merely "temporary proletarians" by accident of birth and will not live out their lives among such squalor. To such persons the "American dream" of upward mobility is very real, and most of them will realize that dream. Anyone can cite numerous examples of persons who arrive in America virtually penniless yet go on to achieve great success, in spite of not even knowing how to speak English. Furthermore, these successes are not unique to some long-vanished age but are repeated by thousands who arrive on these shores every year. These are the true acheivers, the lifeblood of the American economic miracle. This is a profound embarrassment to the resentful, who would prefer to pretend that upward mobility does not exist or is, at best, a fluke. By contrast, there are also countless examples of persons born right here who understand English perfectly yet insist that others pay their bills throughout their entire lifetimes, despite laws that in many cases discriminate in their favor. These are the profoundly resentful, who feel nothing but animosity and contempt for those who support them.

Here in the U.S., many people actually profess to believe that we have no social classes. In truth, we have deliberately blurred the class lines a bit because of a widespread sensitivity about such matters. But no intelligent person can deny that social classes exist. What we have here, however, which is a little unusual historically, are fluid social classes. One does not necessarily spend one's whole life in the social class one is born into. While it is true that the majority does not change social classes significantly, a sizable minority does—and not always for the better, for we have both upward and downward mobility.

What characterizes an identifiable social class is a shared set of values. People within a class tend to have similar views on money and work, on art, on marriage and sex; and they tend to select leisure pursuits from a common "basket." One's social class is not necessarily the class of people into which one is born; rather, it is the class of people whose values most closely match one's own. Marx had the germ of a good idea when he said that class determines consciousness, although he had the causality reversed.[8] "Consciousness" (i.e., values) causes social class by determining one's competence to generate wealth.

SOCIAL CLASSES

One does not need to be truly wealthy to be perceived as a member of the higher classes or to act, think, and feel like one. Those who adopt higher-class values and ethics will find themselves gradually accumulating so much money that no one will doubt their status any longer. The same is true in the other direction. One does not have to be a third-generation welfare mother to be a member in good standing of the underclass. People who adopt underclass values, such as their attitudes about work, money, and what is right and wrong, are unable to maintain a decent living because they cannot hold on to a job. Any tangible assets they may have that are not repossessed for nonpayment will quickly be sold off, and any money left will often be spent on gambling, drinking, or drugs.

Thus we see that the social class one is born into is almost irrelevant. Given a set of values corresponding roughly to those of a particular class, one will rise or fall more or less automatically to where one's income matches one's values pertaining to work and investment. Indeed, this is almost inevitable; there is no way to hold a person in a social class above or below that in which his values place him. Social theorists have not yet learned the futility of such efforts. Trying to raise or lower social classes is like trying to raise or lower the water level on one side of a leaky dike; you can keep pumping the water level up or down, but it is a fundamentally hopeless effort. As soon as the pump stops or slows down (translation: no additional money is available for social programs), everything quickly reverts to the state it would have been at had you done nothing.

I said that where one starts is almost irrelevant. Let me clarify. It truly is almost irrelevant what one's class is at birth, given the enormous possible differentials in one's lifetime earnings. We do not start out with a social class. However, we do start out with parents and other family members. Parents generally give us—in addition to genes—values. Indeed, much of child-raising is concerned with inculcating what are believed to be "correct" values. This fact alone is the principal reason that membership in social classes is believed by some observers to be fixed by heredity. There is no "establishment" keeping the poor "in their place"; the poor do that to each other most effectively through the rigid enforcement of achievement-hating, lower-class values. The fact that children of the lower classes are bombarded with lower-class values every day of their lives suffices to explain why so few of them ever accomplish anything. The powerful resentments within the lower classes, which punish deviation from norms with not only verbal abuse but frequently with physical violence, act as exceedingly powerful deterrents to upward mobility.

Different classes seldom understand each other, although not for the reasons that Marxists assert. The problem is that classes judge each others' actions by the standards that prevail in their own circles. Much of the lower-class outlook is dominated by mistrust, xenophobia, and suspicion. Such an outlook is generally necessary as it confers survival advantage. In proletarian areas, bitter experience gradually teaches that one cannot trust one's neighbors not to steal one's things. Frequently one cannot even trust one's own family members. When the lower classes see examples of generosity on the part of the affluent, they invariably assume that it is some sort of trick. "They must be getting ready to cheat us; why else would they be so nice?" As time passes, and they see that the benificence is real, they then conclude that the upper classes must be impossibly stupid, for why else would anyone just give something away? This encourages them to demand even more generosity from those seemingly foolish folk, just to see if they can get it. All too often, they can.

The same problem occurs in the opposite direction when productive people contemplate the situation of the unproductive. They know that nearly everyone in their own circles genuinely wants to contribute to the general well-being, if given the chance, for this is only fair. Therefore, don't the poor feel likewise? When people in their own circles complain about unfair treatment, it is usually with some justification; is it not the same with the poor? It never occurs to them that some people attempt to live by their wits day by day, never planning, never striving toward any goal, utilizing falsehood and their ability to inspire pity to eke out a meager living free from all personal responsibility. The fact that neither they nor their friends would ever do such a thing wrongly persuades them that no one else would ever do it.

Here in the U.S. we are somewhat unique in that we have two leisure classes: a small one at the top, as most societies have, and a much larger one at the bottom. The leisured underclass does not live opulently, being supported primarily by the largesse of the taxpaying middle class. These are people who have never disciplined themselves to develop the skills needed to get a job that could lift them up from the bottom, and we permit them to collect an income for doing nothing that is comparable to what they would get from honest labor (indeed, in some cases even exceeding it). This privilege is usually passed on to their children. We have allowed ourselves to be persuaded, at least those of us possessing liberal doses of guilt, that if we did not support these people, they would either riot and burn down our cities or else starve to death in the streets before our very eyes, neither of which we can contemplate without alarm. Of course, nothing of the kind would happen; after a short period of adjustment, they would reluctantly go out and take the available jobs. Because much of our underclass is leisured, it is necessary to bring in foreigners to do the work that our domestic underclass would otherwise be doing. Foreigners, of course, are not eligible to receive welfare, and consequently are rarely unemployed.

The contemporary social scene is considerably more complex than the shades of gray between the higher and lower classes. One subclass seldom discussed is the *urban bohemian,* which is typically found only in major cities. In places like New York and San Francisco they constitute a substantial percentage of the population. These people tend to be college educated, highly cultivated in their tastes, but not affluent (often downright poor), and profoundly resentful against wealth and economic achievement. They spend a considerable portion of their time patronizing the fine arts and seeing avant-garde films. They typically do not marry or if they do, have no children. They live in rented apartments and seldom, if ever, put down deep roots of any kind. They are often very active politically and identify almost exclusively with the politics of resentment. They can be counted on with virtual certainty to support any candidate or issue seeking to transfer money from those who earn it to those who covet it from afar.

Urban bohemians are nearly always well educated although typically in subjects that seldom offer the prospect for affluence—

literature, sociology, and so on. Unfortunately for them, they are sharing a city with some extremely motivated and productive people: successful lawyers, accountants, corporate executives, and other professionals who bid up the prices of all commodities, especially housing. Even many blue-collar workers earn far more than do the urban bohemians, adding to the resentment of the latter. "Why should we, whose education is so complete and whose taste is so refined, have to struggle so hard just to live in tiny, shabby, old rented apartments, when many people with far less education than us earn far more?" To make matters worse, the professionals, whose education may be good but whose tastes can sometimes be abominable, can actually afford those conspicuous, expensive condominiums. Oh, rage and envy!

But instead of resolving to compete on equal terms with motivated achievers, these urban bohemians seek the easier path of attempting to defeat their rivals through resentment-oriented political action. Thus, they agitate for rent-control laws that will make it unnecessary for them to compete with achievers for housing. To solve their more fundamental problem—that of having to compete for all goods and services—they promote socialism, which is a generalized form of achiever-control, and the preferred solution of failures worldwide who are sorely vexed by the successful.

Such privation doesn't seem fair—until you realize that the urban bohemians have chosen a lifestyle and an educational pursuit that is far more agreeable to them than the often dreary and stressful ones that many others must endure while pursuing material success. They have decided that the pursuit of art, and "socially relevant" activity is far more important to them than money. That is fine; the choice is theirs. But seeing the money and power that others have makes them forget this and excites a powerful envy, resulting in a lifetime devoted to the politics of resentment.

The situation is much the same in universities, where a highly educated, achievement-oriented academic class faces great competitive pressures to secure and retain positions that for the most part pay very little. Again, it is a question of having made the very personal choice to pursue a certain type of work that is intensely interesting to those who specialize in it, in spite of, not because of, the money they can earn in it. While a few professors in the top schools are paid quite well, going into academia is not a promising way to pursue wealth. There is nothing wrong with deciding that the pleasure of the work performed is more important to one than the disadvantage of dismally low pay. That is everyone's choice to make. But, having made that choice, they have no right to complain when they see others, who have taken no vow of poverty, making far more money than themselves.

The Austrian-born economist Ludwig Von Mises had much to say about resentment in *The Anti-Capitalist Mentality,* a work that was profoundly influenced by Nietzsche (even down to the "dithyrambs" of Dionysius). Von Mises attributes the "resentment of frustrated ambition" of many professionals primarily to envy of their more successful colleagues, who enjoy far more in terms of rewards and public recognition, yet toward whom any overt envy or ill-mannered behavior would be seen as inappropriate and utterly unprofessional. Thus, the intellectual blames capitalism—the system that gives to each no more and no less than what he has earned—for his rage over his own frustrated ambition. In a meritocratic society, says Von Mises, "each member whose ambitions have not been fully satisfied resents the fortune of those who have succeeded better. The fool releases these feelings in slander and defamation. The more sophisticated do not indulge in personal calumny. They sublimate their hatred into a philosophy, the philosophy of anti-capitalism, in order to render inaudible the inner voice that tells them that their failure is entirely their own fault."[9]

I think this is largely correct, but I suspect that a far more potent component of this rage is the intellectuals' anger at seeing blue-collar people, who are less educated than themselves, frequently making more money and enjoying a standard of living that these academics and artists envy. "So unjust this capitalism must be," they reason, "to give a good income to such a clod and so little to a bright fellow like me."

However, two important considerations are often overlooked. First, the high income of many unskilled blue-collar workers is not a phenomenon of capitalism but of the political power wielded by labor unions who have essentially established a legal monopoly in the provision of manual labor. Without the ultimate threat of union or government violence against those who would undercut the union's rates, these high-income blue-collar workers would quickly see their pay fall to the free-market value of their skill (or lack thereof). Second, as noted above, many intellectuals have chosen their field because of their enjoyment of it, not because of its pay. This was a conscious decision to place aesthetic over monetary concerns and is not to be faulted in any way. All of us must make such choices for ourselves. However, the blue-collar worker, who in many cases becomes quite skilled over time and has thus earned the right to a sizeable income, never made any decision to eschew earnings for aesthetics, which thereby renders the comparison invalid.

Von Mises attributes the "anti-capitalistic bias of American intellectuals" primarily to the fact that they generally have no opportunity to interact with "high society" (or, as it is called in France, *le monde*), which European intellectuals more typically do. Hence, he says, this bias is "more general and more bitter" in the United States than in Europe, where access to "society" is "open to anyone who has distinguished himself in any field." While this may have been true in the 1950s when Von Mises was writing, I doubt if American intellectuals are significantly more anti-capitalist today than European ones; I suspect that the reverse may even be true. In any case, American and European intellectuals both suffer from the "status inconsistency" of high education, training, and competitiveness but only modest income, which is a combination likely to produce significant resentment against the economic system that they feel fails to recognize their very real, but unmarketable, merit.

Marx's nightmare has at last been realized. The size of the bourgeoisie in industrialized countries has grown to include most of the population, thereby making it vastly harder for resentment to seize total control. Much of that group, especially its higher achievers, share most of the characteristics that were once ear-marks of the aristocracy: an appreciation of education, the arts, and culture; a tolerant and cosmopolitan world-view; and an insistence on treating everyone with magnanimity and fairness, even in instances where it will not be reciprocated. They are shocked by revelations of wrongdoing in high places. They are clearly the contemporary "truthful ones." The vast majority of the population has, frankly, no sympathy whatsoever for communism. However, resentment against outstanding achievers still persists in many areas, owing to the deeply ingrained Christian notion that the poor are "the good"—a notion which is largely responsible for the success of a secular Christian morality, i.e., socialism.

The problems of the lower classes, with which any sensitive person can easily sympathize on an emotional level, are an inevitable consequence of the achievement-hating values these people preserve and transmit. Achievement is required to generate income and wealth, but achievement is no more able to take root in that environment than is a rain forest in a desert. Unfortunately, instead of teaching us to reject these wretched achievement-hating values, the prevailing Christian/Marxist morality teaches us to exalt them as the highest ideal. Instead of feeling revolted and shocked by the people who hold them, we are taught to revere these people as the truly blessed, the unselfish, the people closest to God. And if such "unselfish" behavior is the highest ideal, why should I, or anyone else, strive to achieve anything productive? Why should we all not pursue that worthiest ideal, poverty? Should I not drop out of school, sign up for welfare, and demand to have all my needs automatically met by some hard-working capitalist exploiter? The less I strive to fulfill my own needs, the more worthy I am in this view of having them met at someone else's expense.

Obviously, as that system of morality is pursued, the number of achievers declines at the same time that the number of the nonworking resentful increases, and at some point the society crumbles. Civilization is the sum total of all its achievements, and as achievement is increasingly scorned, civilization itself slows, then stops, and finally collapses. If we wish to preserve civilization, let alone see it advance, we must not view *les miserables* of the lower classes with wonder and awe, seeing in them the embodiment of all that is pure and unselfish. Instead, we must face up to reality and see them as the failures they really are, while recognizing that they are not totally beyond the possibility of improvement should they ever "re-valuate" their values. The values of the lower classes, as celebrated in Christian/Marxist ethics, are not the highest possible ideal; they represent problems to be overcome.

NOTES

1. Nietzsche, *The Genealogy of Morals* (1887), first essay, sections 4, 5, 7.
2. Nietzsche, *Beyond Good and Evil* (1886), section 260. One point that is misunderstood by nearly everyone concerns what is supposed to lie "Beyond Good and Evil." The prevailing interpretation is, in essence, "anything goes"; that all standards of morality are tossed out the window, and that you are free to make up any that you choose. This is incorrect. Nietzsche sought to "re-valuate" standards of morality, not to abolish them. When we pass beyond the Christian-derived standards of "Good and Evil," with their emphasis on passivity (which Nietzsche scornfully terms "slave morality"), we pass into what he calls "noble morality" (or "master morality"), where the active virtues predominate. This is nicely summarized in R. J. Hollingdale's Appendix to his English translation of Nietzsche's *Twilight of the Idols* and *The Anti-Christ* (New York: Penguin Books, 1968).
3. Quoted in *Thomas Jefferson On Democracy,* edited by Saul K.

SOCIAL CLASSES

Padover (Englewood Cliffs, N.J.: D. Appleton-Century, 1939).

4. Arendt, Hannah, *Totalitarianism* (New York: Harcourt, Brace, & World, 1968), chapter 3, part 3.

5. Morality as strength: *Human, All Too Human,* section 93. "Competent to promise": *The Genealogy of Morals,* second essay, section 2.

6. Axelrod, Robert, *The Evolution of Economic Cooperation* (New York: Basic Books, 1984). See also the article "Could Hobbes Trounce Hayek?" by Joseph P. Martino in the February, 1985 issue of *Reason.*

7. Lewis, Oscar, *Children of Sanchez* (New York: Random House, 1961). *La Vida* (New York: Irvington, 1983). Interestingly, despite his accurate portrayal of the wretched failure-oriented lifestyle of the proletariat, Lewis remained a devout socialist. He must somehow have convinced himself that these people, who as individuals were so frequently unreliable, untruthful, and vicious, would nonetheless rule collectively with magnanimity and justice (unless, like so many socialists, what Lewis was actually seeking was not justice but revenge).

8. Marx, Karl, *Critique of Political Economy* (1859), preface. "It is not the consciousness of men that determines their existence, but on the contrary it is their social existence that determines their consciousness."

9. Von Mises, Ludwig, *The Anti-Capitalist Mentality* (Princeton, New Jersey: Van Nostrand Reinhold, 1956), pp. 11-17.

3.

Resentment and Education

Education is more than just the dissemination of facts to the young. It is an attempt to instill achievement-oriented values in youth and to make them active participants in the civilization in which they will spend the rest of their lives. Some of today's youth will grow up to be great surgeons, concert pianists, architects, or inventors. Still others will build houses, fix plumbing, or bake pizzas; and all of these achievements, large and small, will make up the civilization in which our children will live. The attempt to educate our youth is one of our noblest actions. Education can be misused, as when it is warped into dubious or dishonest propaganda. But when pursued in good faith, education shows the human race at its finest.

That education seeks to do far more than just teach useful

facts can readily be seen in the curriculum of any high school or college. Students are introduced to the fine arts, to great literature, to history, and to philosophy, all of which are useless in the economic sense but invaluable for an understanding of civilization. These are undeniably upper-class values; only a small percentage of the adult population can coherently discuss the nuances of literary criticism or the historical and political ramifications of battles, yet an attempt is made to teach these earmarks of aristocracy to all students. A democratic capitalist society cannot predict what social class its future leaders will come from; it must take them where it finds them. Seeds must be sown everywhere, to take root where they may. The soil may be much more fertile in some areas than others, but at least a few splendid flowers will be found in all regions. To earn the intellectual and financial rewards of a proper education requires, of course, competence, diligence, and disciplined effort, all of which are values which characterize productive people. The values that characterize unproductive people—resentment, intolerance, and inertia—will, when prevalent, propagate total ignorance. So when we attempt to teach lower-class youth anything at all, it is in a very real sense an assault on lower-class culture by the upper classes. We are trying to make the lower classes disappear by recruiting all of its members into the upper classes. This has actually been occurring, albeit very slowly, for at least the past two centuries: Millions of today's middle and even upper-class people were born to impoverished parents or grandparents, and used education as a ladder to get where they are today.

This "assault" on lower-class culture is not done out of sinister motives, but out of a very sincere benificence. The natural tendency for achievers is to help others succeed. They never fully understand why some people never succeed in anything they undertake. Achievers work under the assumption that everyone will succeed if only given the chance; for does not everyone want to improve his life? Thus, as long as there are failures, many achievers assume that it must mean that those people were never offered a chance for success. The notion that the poor are simply living in accordance with their own lower-class values never occurs to achievers. Achievers reason that no one would ever choose poverty; therefore, these people must never have been given any other choice. Of course, no one deliberately chooses poverty, but many do wish idly for affluence without choosing to develop those traits which make affluence attainable: self-discipline, careful planning, and scrupulous honesty. This inevitably results in frustration and hence profound resentment; for a clear understanding and appreciation of cause-and-effect is widespread only among the productive. Just as the path we take has consequences for us, so too does the path not taken; so the failure to develop achievement-oriented habits and skills early in life amounts to a choice to live in poverty, albeit by default.

The large industry of education exists to allow this benign cultural imperialism to happen. Even the parents of lower-class children almost invariably approve of the attempt, themselves recognizing the desirability of their children holding productive values instead of the prevailing slum ethics. Unfortunately, most parents in lower-class areas seldom follow through on it with enough persistence, diligence, and home support to ensure long-term success. Fortunately, a significant number of them do, and their children leave behind the poverty, filth, and crime typical of the proletarian existence and enter the middle classes. In some cases, they rise all the way to the top.

One would think that virtually all young people from poor families would eagerly embrace any institution that offered them (free of charge) the opportunity to escape the misery of the slums. While at least some do, for most of them the situation is precisely the opposite. Schools in slum areas of inner cities are typically in what might be called a state of war with their students. Violence is common; and teachers, instead of being honored and sought out as mentors, are frequently vilified, harassed, and threatened. Heated defiance of the school's rules is the norm, even when the most reasonable of rules are enforced sparingly and with a light touch. Many lower-class youth positively bristle like porcupines with the sharp quills of resentment. For most of these students, becoming educated is the last thing on their minds. They diligently strive not to become learned or successful, but to become ultimately "cool."

What is the essence of this state called "cool," to which many so fervently aspire? It is a conspicuous display of flamboyant perversity, frequently overflowing into destructiveness, which is hostile to all things associated with achievement. It is the enforcement mechanism of the values of the lower classes, the glue that holds the slums together. This idealization of lower-class values is what limits the number of people who achieve upward mobility and keeps the poor in their place. If one has become totally "cool," one possesses a set of resentments that has been polished to an unbelievably high degree: One dramatically scorns all things associated with the morality of achievement. One savors not accomplishment, but especially flamboyant displays of perversity.

For one who aspires to the very heights of coolness, one must never be seen attempting to succeed academically. Every word spoken, every action, and every gesture must be scrutinized for possible insults—real or imagined. One must above all never fail to behave abrasively toward anyone who does not share one's resentments, or who is more successful, more intelligent, or more productive than oneself. To behave in a civil manner toward "the man" (i.e., those who are identified with the productive building and running of our civilization) is unthinkable; that would be fraternization with the enemy. When scrutiny is lax, violence against such people is appropriate, even encouraged. To be fully "cool" is to explicitly and emphatically reject all achievement-oriented values, especially disciplined work and civilized behavior. It is a weapon in widespread use in the "class war."

To be "cool" is to be the antithesis of an eager young worker who is anxious to succeed. Sufficiently "cool" people, should they have a job at all, are certain to be miserable workers. At work they will display surly demeanors, never giving more than minimal and reluctant compliance to their boss's requests. Often it is necessary to make a show of not obeying the boss's orders before actually doing so. (I have observed this occasionally in stores and restaurants.) Should such people be seen by any of their co-workers in the act of actually being helpful or eager in their work, their reputation for being "cool" will be shattered. By striving to be "cool" in all things, they will be promotion-proofed for life. They will occupy the bottom rung of the ladder forever—assuming they don't fall off the ladder completely. To strive mightily to enhance, expand, and perfect one's resentments can truly be called the "will to poverty".

RESENTMENT AND EDUCATION

In school it is especially necessary to be "cool." The teachers are attempting to instill aristocratic values: a love of learning, a knowledge of mathematics, science, art, history, and so on. But the resentful see such learning as oppression that is not to be tolerated. It may be resisted by cutting class, or by attending but making trouble in some creative way. Violence is helpful, because it totally obliterates the highly refined atmosphere of trust and mutual support that is essential for learning. If one's resentment against the successful achiever is strong enough, it will guarantee one's failure not only in school, but throughout life.

If you have the misfortune to be born into a low-income area, there are powerful chains holding you in the poverty lifestyle: your fellow slummers, who will show no mercy if you are insufficiently "cool." The least of your problems will be the names they call you every time they see you. You may be able to ignore this if you are strong enough. Much harder to ignore are the cruel and often vicious attacks by juvenile toughs or by whole gangs of toughs (for *le proletarianisme n'oblige pas:* no Marquis of Queensberry rules here) against young males who do not conform by displaying readily visible resentment against school and work. Every time they spot you, you are fair game, for you are perceived as part of the group that they are resentful against—the competent. They typically do not have the opportunity to "work over" the principal of the school or the "rich" man who runs the supermarket. But *you* are within their reach. Because of the prospect of forever trying to evade the attacks of one's fellow slummers, growing up under such vicious harassment is dreadful. The career of many a young would-be achiever is cut short at an early age: "Hey, man, don't mess with me, I'm cool, too." And thus begins another life of poverty. But notice that it is not the "greedy capitalists" who perpetuate the poverty of the lower classes. Quite the contrary; they are doing all they can to help the poor escape it. Poverty is perpetuated by the powerful—even murderous—resentments of those living in the slums, whose feelings of anger are frequently uncontrollable.

Should you survive these attacks, both verbal and physical, and still reach adulthood without conforming to lower-class values, the higher classes will scarcely notice that you have not been with them all along. However, only the strongest individuals can withstand the unrelenting harassment and abuse that are suffered by youth who attempt to rise out of the slums. This is why students in high-income areas almost invariably perform the best in school. The enforcement of underclass values in their neighborhood is weak to nonexistent. Whatever virtues the school itself may have are second-order effects. As long as a school meets certain minimal standards, which most (although perhaps not all) American schools do, the educational outcome will be determined primarily by the social class of the students enrolled— i.e., the degree of resentfulness among the students and their families, or the lack thereof. It matters relatively little how much money is spent on each student. If the student body of a school in a "good" suburban area were exchanged with one in a notorious slum, keeping the schools and faculties the same, people would be amazed by how successful the "bad" school could be.

This also explains why most private schools outperform public schools. Parents who hold fast to lower-class values are unlikely to spend what little money they have to buy a better education for their children, while those who are willing to make that sacrifice—whatever their level of income—are obviously highly supportive of educational goals. In fact, significant numbers of lower-income parents do make extreme sacrifices to give their children a private education. With disciplined, goal-seeking parents like these, their children are virtually certain to succeed. In a very real sense, the tuition paid for attendance at private schools functions like a toll gate, keeping out all but those who value education highly. Even if private schools were to lose much of their tuition-based funds, leaving only the barest pittance to run on, they would nonetheless, in most cases, produce outstanding results because of their exclusion of students from families in which inertia or resentment predominates. Not only do such children nearly always fail to become educated themselves, but they often grievously interfere with the education of others as well. Thus, tuition functions like an impenetrable barrier proclaiming "Resentment Keep Out!"

Another advantage of private schools is that they can set standards both for academic achievement and for behavior, which no public school in the United States is allowed to do. To set a standard of any kind implies the eventual exclusion of those who fail to meet it. However, public schools are required by law to enroll and retain any student who lives in the district, regardless of academic performance or disruptive behavior. Thus, the only quality control possible for consumers of public education is to select a district where the cost of housing is far too high for the profoundly resentful to live.

Students perform best where the obstacles are fewest, and lower-class resentment is the greatest obstacle to educational success everywhere. Consider the happy situation in those prosperous areas where the resentful do not live. Children learn serenely in an environment where achievement is seen as both normal and proper. The role model for youth is not the meanest bully or the most explosively resentful delinquent but the successful scholar or the accomplished athlete. Such schools should be seen not as targets of resentful envy but as examples of what is possible—indeed, what should be expected as the norm—in a civilized society. While there are no easy solutions to the major problems facing public schools in many areas today, it is clear that one key element of the solution will have to be to separate the profoundly resentful from the achievers, at least until such time as they learn to keep their resentments under control. To continue to warehouse them there out of some sense of misguided egali-tarianism is a major error, for not only does it render them more resentful than ever but it severly interferes with the education of those who are eager to learn. (And even in the poorest areas a significant number of students would succeed if they were not hindered by their more resentful peers.)

The undisciplined poor are generally unsuccessful in most of the efforts they undertake, and this is especially true in the most trying yet vital of human tasks: child-raising. Being a parent of small children—especially several very young children at the same time—places one in a state of long-term, unrelieved stress; and difficulty in handling stress is one highly visible characteristic of the underclass. They frequently react to stress with arbitrary violence and brutality, a reflection of their very real state of generalized confusion. Domestic violence is frequently the norm in such circles, and many children routinely expect to be beaten from time to time. The lower-class tradition of machismo, which defines masculinity in terms of brutal mayhem, causes achievement to be scorned by males as a feminine trait, since achievers are by nature tolerant and civilized, while "real men" are supposed to be savages. (Achievement is, of course, neuter and color-blind as well.) This is why males tend to perceive those males in the classes above them as effeminate. Achievement-oriented males do not share the lower classes' relish for uncivilized behavior.

This dilemma is compounded in environments where achievement-oriented behavior in males (study, reading, and especially interest in fine art) is considered proof of effeminacy. (And for this reason, how many men, steeped in the notion that males must be savages, but being too intelligent, too sensitive to live that vulgar lifestyle, adopt the sexual identity of females?) It is clear that parents who are failure-prone tend to raise failure-prone children, because raising an intelligent, well-adjusted, and creative child is a task requiring considerable patience, effort, knowledge, and self-control—in other words, upper-class skills. (Observe in a playground in an affluent area how educated mothers strive to enhance their childrens' vocabulary and turn every chance discovery into a learning experience. By contrast, children raised in slum areas rarely experience exercises in vocabulary-building.) The great majority of lower-class parents simply lack the competence to nurture achievement-oriented values in their children, and thus the underclass is perpetuated.

When very young children grow up in an environment that is confusing, chaotic, and randomly threatening and violent, only the most self-directed and disciplined among them will ever rise above such behavior themselves. Consider how difficult it must be for children whose parents are not among the "truthful ones" to acquire a rational view of the world. One day a certain type of behavior meets with approval or is at least tolerated; another day, the same behavior brings a vicious beating with no explanation of why anything changed. Rules are made but change chaotically and are impossible to follow. Promises are made but seldom kept. No examples are to be seen of anyone, anywhere, who achieves a major long-term goal through careful planning, saving, working, or by self-mastery. Good things are attributed to "good luck" and disasters to "bad luck," or possibly even a curse or spell. If you gamble, perhaps today "luck" may favor you. Then you'd be as lucky as the rich folk! No one seems to have a clear appreciation of cause and effect. The criterion for acceptable behavior seems to be: do what you feel like at the moment with no thought of the consequences. Planning for the future is an upper-class skill.

We have not yet mentioned the other major function of education besides disseminating information, a function nearly as important as the first: sorting students by ability. A complex modern society requires this function to be performed, since multitudes of occupations, each requiring a different mix of talent and discipline, exist. Some people have strong talents of the broadest possible scope and are fit to be leaders of great enterprises, while others have significant abilities concentrated in certain more narrow fields. Other people have relatively modest abilities but can learn useful skills with training; and still others have virtually no ambition or willingness to learn and can perform only the most menial of tasks. Such classifications are not meaningless or thought up to gratify the ego of a racist or sexist elite, as some imagine. Differences in individuals' abilities to carry out economically useful tasks are every bit as real as individual differences in strength or dexterity.

In rigid societies, where social class is fixed at birth, it is not difficult to "discover" someone's level of ability. Just look at that individual's parents and assume that their children will be carbon copies of them. However, in a meritocratic capitalist society this is not nearly so easy to do, since rare talent may come from even the poorest quarter and mediocrity from the best. History provides us with many examples of leaders in business and politics who began their lives at the bottom.

In the nineteenth and early twentieth centuries, businesses were willing to perform this sorting on their own. An ambitious young man with little formal education might be hired to sort letters in the mailroom and within twenty years be running the company. Today, businesses are exceedingly degree-conscious, perhaps too much so. Personally, I would like to see the flexibility of the old system retained where possible, at least in part; I have seen many examples of people without college degrees learning far more useful skills on the job than did others with impressive academic credentials. Formal education should in general suggest certain career choices, but should not be the only factor in determining those choices.

The work of the education industry allows potential employers to sort students in several ways. Students receive grades in school that reflect mastery of certain subject areas and roughly indicate a student's ability in each subject. Students take standardized tests that reveal very accurately the student's abilities in the areas covered by the test. Also, the overall quantity of education completed provides some rough indication of ability.

The worst students typically do not even finish high school. To complete at least a few years of college indicates a moderately high degree of persistence and ability. To graduate from a respected college with a good academic record indicates considerable ability. To complete a rigorous graduate education indicates even more ability.

Thus disseminating information to students is only one of the useful functions performed by education. The other is to give us a measure, approximate though it is, of a student's ability to achieve, as well as an indication of where a student's strongest abilities lie. For example, when a business interviews a college graduate who has a successful major in mathematics or chemistry, it suggests that this person might make a good computer programmer even if the student has no previous experience in that area. When they interview a high-school dropout, it suggests that he almost certainly will not. Indeed, the sheer number of years of one's education can be used almost as an index of persistence, an indicator of one's willingness to set goals and stay with them. Even if the universities were to teach their students nothing but some rigorous yet utterly useless subject, such as the translation of ancient Mesopotamian cuneiforms into Chinese, they would still be performing a useful task to business by indicating which students are competent to master such a demanding task. That schools can perform this sorting while actually teaching students something useful like mathematics or economics is all to the better.

Education is an extremely difficult undertaking that is often thankless and resentment-provoking but nonetheless indispensable. The great goal of education should be not only to teach facts and sort students by ability but also to instill a love of great thought and noble action. Education seeks to recruit all youth to the ranks of the "truthful ones," even though it knows it cannot always succeed. Education continues to be offered to all, even though there are many who refuse it and more than a few who actually assault the very people who are trying to provide it to them. The result of one's encounter with education tells the world, which knows nothing of one as an individual, the degree to which one has acquired self-mastery.

Whether a school is public or private matters less than the degree to which that school can set and enforce standards. In the present political environment, private schools have all the advantages because the resentful have made it impossible for the public schools to enforce academic and behavioral standards, since, when students are sorted by achievement, children from resentment-oriented groups turn up predominantly at the bottom. Resentment's predictable answer to this problem is to blame achievement and to deny the desirability of educational success and/or the validity of the measurements thereof. "Failure is just as good as success," grumble the resentful, "except in the eyes of the ruling class." But we cannot claim to love our culture, our accomplishments, our arts and sciences, or any of civilization's fine achievements when we say it is as acceptable for students to fail as it is for them to succeed. No, we must admit that it is better to succeed than to fail, or else it is a waste of time and effort to even try to educate anyone. Having admitted this, we must conclude that we are right to accord special honor and recognition to those who have disciplined themselves to succeed. We must likewise admit that those who succeed in education are for the most part justified in their expectation of enjoying greater economic rewards than those who do not: for if all must be equal, then why should anyone ever strive to succeed? And if no one strives to succeed, then what becomes of civilization?

Those who fail — or worse yet, become abusive of those who succeed — must not be contemplated with reverence and awe, as symbols of society's alleged failure; the failure clearly lies in the values to which they cling, in what they aver to be the "good." It is a consequence of their resentment against achievement. For education to succeed, angry failures must be gently removed from the academic curriculum.

Education is the name given to the attempt to instill the achievement-oriented values characteristic of productive people in all students, regardless of their background. It is the noble attempt to expand the upper classes downward, to go forth to all young people to try to teach them to achieve. Nonetheless, in spite of our best efforts, there will always be some students who can not, or will not, become achievers, and who become abusive of those who are. What can we do with those who cannot become achievers? We must teach them to get out of the way of those who can.

4.

Resentment as an Ideal

Wealth is crime enough to him that's poor
—Sir John Denham (1615-1669)

From an abstract perspective, it would seem highly unlikely that something as ugly as resentment would be elevated to the status of a lofty moral ideal. However, much of the world knows of no higher virtue than to be resentful against the successful achiever. Wherever you see misery and self-denial proclaimed as both necessary and virtuous, you can be certain that it is the voice of resentment speaking, for achievement sings in far happier tones.

A society in which resentment is widely regarded as a virtue is a society at war with itself. It despises its own greatest bene-factors: its achievers, who provide its very means of survival as well as defense against its enemies. When achievers are scorned, despised, or even punished, as they are in Marxist countries, those things that a civilized society needs for its continued survival will be increasingly difficult to come by, since only achievement can provide them. Where resentment prevails, living standards will be far lower than they are in more rational countries where achievement is encouraged. Of course, some reluctant compliance can be extorted from achievement by the free use of the whip and the threat of even worse, but slavery produces only the most menial accomplishments—and even those are only reluctantly yielded up. This explains why socialist economies, which must employ threats instead of promises, always lag far behind their capitalist counterparts. (To "motivate" slaves within their society, the Romans needed the cross, which for centuries represented the ultimate in humiliation and suffering. Its significance was stolen and reversed in the most brilliant semantic coup in all history. To be a surly, noncompliant slave became henceforth not only acceptable, but holy!) There is no escaping the conclusion that economic arrangements based on threats and compulsion are grossly inefficient, as well as immoral.

When resentment reigns as the acknowledged ideal, it is necessary to preach self-denial and resignation to attempt to squelch peoples' perfectly reasonable desires to live rich and full lives. Unfettered human beings naturally try to pursue their own interests in every way they can. When they believe that individual happiness is both possible and desirable, people will naturally strive to achieve it. This requires society's permission—even encouragement—to strive toward goals, the attainment of which not only enriches the individual, but also contributes to the economic and cultural well-being of the community. By disciplining oneself to achieve a desirable goal, by working hard in one's own self-interest, one gradually achieves a state of prosperity and security that is conducive to long-term happiness.

Resentment, however, must stop people from pursuing their own happiness too diligently, lest they become too attached to the fruits of achievement. Thus happiness itself, which is both the rationale for and the consequence of achievement, must be poisoned. It must be drowned in that lower-class venom, suspicion. "The apparent happiness of the prosperous is not real," resentment preaches. "You think you see it, but it is really just temporary, an illusion. They are all sinners, and they will be punished in the afterlife (or in the Revolution)." However, if people believe that the happiness of material success is, or can be, real, they will pursue it as a goal, and resentment will have nothing to offer them.

The very cornerstone of Christian values is misery, with its doctrine that the world must necessarily be a "vale of tears." Not only is earthly human happiness not possible, but it is positively sinful to even try to attain it. Those who strive to obtain wealth to satisfy material wants or indulge in worldly, sensual pleasures will be punished by God for seeking to enjoy this life instead of waiting for their reward in the next. One must deny oneself all earthly pleasures in order to enjoy the pleasures promised in the afterlife. If one is faced with poverty and hardship, one must face it with resignation, and turn the other cheek to earthly affronts.

In the neo-Christian morality of Marxism, which shares the grim outlook on life of the lower classes, the emphasis is much the same. When people want to know why it is not possible to enjoy the simple worldly pleasures of consumer goods and small luxuries, which are abundant in capitalist countries, the response is that these are decadent bourgeois pleasures that are unproletarian (i.e., sinful) to enjoy. Those who are enjoying such pleasures today are all capitalist sinners who will soon be punished by proletarian uprisings. You must sacrifice today: you must work harder to build socialism, without asking for anything for yourself in return. When the final glorious victory of the working classes has been achieved, there will be great happiness and abundant prosperity for all. But until that time, we must continue to sacrifice.

Bourgeois achievement, on the other hand, offers the prospect of happiness not in some far-off and probably imaginary place or time but in the here and now. Furthermore, many people can be seen enjoying their rewards today—a demonstration of promises delivered that neither Christianity nor Marxism can provide. Consequently, when earthly happiness is philosophically believed to be possible, it follows that people will strive to obtain it. Thus, for resentment to stop people from following their normal inclinations to pursue material success, it is necessary to preach constant sacrifice and self-denial; to quench the very desire for happiness itself.

The Christians' rage against others' sexual pleasure is just another manifestation of their hatred and envy of worldly pleasure, for no other pursuit promises such purely earthly enjoyment and delivers on its promise so quickly. Life's greatest failures (the profoundly repressed, those warped with revengefulness, the unsanitary) contemplate the sexual enjoyment of those more for-

tunate than themselves with powerful but repressed envy, which
leads to great anger. "How dare anyone be happy and healthy,
free of guilt, and be blessed with such worldly joy? How dare
they be untroubled by the fear and guilt which plagues me? How
dare anyone be happy when I am not?" Marxists also share
this Christian attitude, displaying their hatred of worldly pleasure
by denouncing all overt sensuality as "bourgeois decadence" and
suppressing all erotic magazines, books, and performances as
vehemently as any Victorian bluenose.

At the dawn of the twentieth century, socialism was seen
as a great liberating ideal. It was believed that socialism, when
realized, would once and for all bring the world liberty, an end
to oppression, general prosperity, great art, literature, and so
on. Visionaries like H. G. Wells, George Bernard Shaw, Bertrand
Russell, Sinclair Lewis, Edward Bellamy, and many others
suggested that the only obstacle to an earthly Utopia was the
continued existence of capitalism, and that a benign, liberating
socialism was the only solution. Reading the work of these writers,
it is impossible to mistake the sincerity of their convictions or
the innocence of their intentions. Socialism would transform the
world into a garden in which all countries and all classes would
live in peace; and science would raise everyone's living standards
beyond our wildest dreams.

Today, virtually no one who is free to speak his mind says
this. We have all seen socialism, and it is anything but pleasant.
In the real world, socialism is invariably squalid, repressive,
shabby, militaristic, and mendacious. It would be generally admitted today, even by most socialists, that socialism will not provide the same degree of material prosperity associated with capital-

ism. At best, socialism promises a shabby egalitarian existence in which all equally share cramped housing and wait in long lines for scarce consumer goods: In the absence of generous loans and other assistance from capitalist countries, the result could be even worse.

And socialism *certainly* will not bring us freedom. It would further be admitted by most socialists today that government restrictions on individual liberties (including the freedom to change jobs, to exchange possessions and services, to live where one wants, and especially the freedom to question the wisdom of state planners) must be increased significantly under socialism. Nor will the fine arts thrive under socialism, as was once believed, for all hands and all minds must serve the goals of the state— goals that are determined by an all-powerful leader, who must not be questioned. Artists are told what kind of art is needed by the state!

Yet even while recognizing this dismal picture, many people *still want socialism,* even though they know it will unquestionably make us less free, less prosperous, and less cultured than we are now. What possible motivation could they have? Many nineteenth-century socialists clearly were striving to promote human happiness, however misguidedly. Socialism was mistakenly associated with science, technology, art, and progress. The reality is that socialist countries are years behind the capitalist West in science and technology; that they are incapable of manufacturing consumer items of good enough quality to export; and that creative artists are in chains. So what could possibly motivate today's socialists to see this squalid failure as something worth struggling for? What do they value? It is clearly not human happiness, for everyone can see that socialism brings nothing but squalor and misery. It certainly is not liberty. Can it be anything other than the envy and hatred of achievement, the desire to end the happiness of those who currently enjoy it? Can socialism be anything other than resentment against achievement?

It must be noted, however, that at least some achievers are themselves partly to blame for the widespread rejection of the morality of achievement, because to them achievement is a wretched duty, rather than a fitting outlet for their own creative energies. Some forms of achievement are pursued purely for monetary reasons, some for personal satisfaction, and some for a combination of both. But the dismal-faced achiever, who may be very successful in his own career, sees nothing but sacrifice and suffering in work and furthermore believes achievement to be incompatible with happiness: if you're enjoying yourself, then you are not working hard enough. To take a vacation is suspect, to pursue outside interests or spend time with one's family is a sign of weakness. This of course is the Calvinist outlook, which is a compromise between Christianity and achievement. Retaining the Christian doctrine of original sin and the need for suffering, it equates work with punishment, seeing work as a kind of self-denial. Is it any wonder that achievement has enemies when even some of its friends promote it like this?

High-technology "startup companies" in Silicon Valley and elsewhere typically display these traits, which explains why so few of them ever achieve long-term success. Mature and experienced professionals (those people whose productivity is the very highest) will not tolerate this lifestyle indefinitely. This causes the startup companies to lose out to larger, well-established companies, which consider vacations, outside interests, and family life normal. The equation of work with suffering, the insistence that one's employment must squeeze out all of life's other pursuits: do we not hear in this echoes of the Christian's mortification of the flesh, the equation of pain with virtue? Even in achievement we sometimes encounter the premise that we are put on earth to suffer. But the dismal-faced achiever, common as he is, need not be the norm. He is a product of a religious and cultural tradition that promotes suffering as a virtue, but he has at least been wise enough to direct his negative impulses into positive channels. To be sure, it is better than nailing one's hands to a cross or sleeping on a block of wood. As the influence of religion decreases and life gradually becomes more joyous, we can expect to see less of this person. Achievement should be pursued to enhance one's enjoyment of life, not to undermine it.

We must be careful never to imply a minimum threshold for achievement by disparaging all who fall short of it. To do so merely forces those people into resentment's camp: "I tried to do my best, but they said it wasn't good enough." Instead, we must encourage and welcome all sincere attempts at achievement, no matter how modest; for sometimes great achievers start out with modest beginnings. Modest achievement brings only modest rewards, but far better this than a lifetime on the dole. Furthermore, each individual must make his own decisions on balancing the need for income versus other pursuits, and the right choice for one person may not be right for someone else. As long as people are paying their own way, we have no grounds for criticizing their choices.

The main impediment to the growth and proliferation of

achievement-oriented values, and consequently to the advance of civilization, is the profound anti-achievement bias in Western society. Its roots are in Christianity—that momentous victory of resentful ignorance over the commerce and learning of the ancient world. Unapologetic and uncompromising Christianity consists of virtually 100 percent resentment-morality. It may be more than a coincidence that those ethnic groups that today appear to be the most successful—the Japanese and the Jews— have not had the dubious benefit of a Christian education. It may also be more than a coincidence that the ethnic groups that have traditionally displayed the most fervent and uncritical religiosity—blacks and Hispanics—are on the average among the lowest in achievement. It should surprise no one that children raised on the nostrum "Blessed are the Poor" will be unwilling to expend much effort to escape beatitude.

Nearly everyone in our society is steeped in Christianity and Christian-derived values from the earliest childhood. However, even those who are eventually able to throw off belief in Christian theology usually remain steeped in Christian morality, which accounts for the spectacular success of Marx's expropriation of Christ's morality. Only those of the keenest intellect succeed in freeing themselves not only from their belief in the childish legends about the creation, the flood, the virgin birth, the resurrection, and the like, but from the stranglehold of a morality teaching that those who are the greatest failures in life exemplify the highest ideal.

The late and unlamented belief system of fascism also ideal- ized resentment against success. Hitler primarily exploited the resentment that Germans felt against the victorious Allies of the

RESENTMENT AS AN IDEAL

First World War. (That the Allies were unnecessarily harsh and not magnanimous in their victory, I do not deny. However, resentment exists even when the stronger party is virtuous to a fault; it is the result of weakness confronting strength, not of the abuse of strength.) Hitler combined this with the long-simmering undercurrent of resentment against the prosperous but "foreign believing" Jews that ran throughout Europe. The result was a national insanity, the ultimate romantic intoxication of nationalist and racialist thinking, a poisonous witches' brew that ultimately led to death for tens of millions and ruin for Europe.

In many segments of society, there is no higher moral principle known than profound resentment against success. Many pious Christians spend every Sunday morning renouncing material success, and then the next five or six days pursuing it. Many university professors sanctimoniously pontificate against the material success of achievers and bewail the privations of the terminally inept, then throw themselves into a fanatically intense competition for professional advancement and recognition.

What do we call those people who have no job skills or self-discipline whatsoever? "The blessed," if we are Christians; "victims of capitalism," if we are socialists. Yet how many liberal professors would be willing to accept street people as peers and colleagues in their professional endeavors? On what grounds could they then deny corporations the right to make the same rational decision? Let those who have never discriminated against incompetence in their own field cast the first stone. Granting that standards are necessary, then who is to blame for the wretchedness of life's failures? Can it be that no one's greed is at fault, and that such people simply bring misfortune upon themselves through their system of values because they are unable or unwilling to accept the discipline of the workplace? But that is a forbidden thought, a conclusion that no socialist dare entertain for even a moment. How can there ever be a classless society if some classes of people drive themselves like dynamos pursuing and planning for success, while others wallow in whiskey and drugs complaining about their "bad luck?"

The notion that people are themselves in any way responsibile for their own well-being, or lack thereof, is poisonous to Christian and socialist values alike; for once we admit that the affluent have earned their wealth, we have no justification for envy of them. Therefore, the resentful must pretend that there was no choice, that they are not themselves to blame for their own failures.

One very common outlet for expressing the morality of re-sentment is through organized protests of every kind: marching, demonstrating, chanting, and so on. The politics of resentment make good use of the freedoms granted by tolerant achievement even to those who oppose it—freedoms which would instantly vanish should resentment actually come to power. It need not be the case that all protest implies resentment, even though it usually works out that way. There are perfectly legitimate things to protest from the pro-achievement, pro-freedom, and tolerance position. For example, such protests might be aimed at reducing the amount of money stolen from the paychecks of working people to support the nonworking resentful, or they might be aimed against government restrictions on our liberties, or against human rights violations in countries less tolerant than our own. However, protest today is primarily the province of the resentful, and it is not difficult to see why. For one thing, protest is definitely a low-paying activity. In many instances it is simply a waste of time, while in other circumstances it yields results only after prodigious expenditures of time spent in organization and protest.

Achievers are people who accomplish much in a small amount of time, and if there is one thing the achiever is always short of, it is time. The demands of running a business or professional career are so draining on one's time and energy that one is extremely limited in what outside activities one can take on. Given the choice between joining some probably futile protest or doing something that will be far more pleasant or will yield far more gain, the achiever sees little point in wasting his time in a march. But the resentful—many of whom are living on various government handouts—have far more time on their hands and far fewer concerns about productive activity. Hence they are free to dissipate their time in this manner without remorse. Others are university students or faculty, who work hard at times but have long breaks and summers free. (How many high-earning achievers will ever have a whole summer free?) One left-wing social activist, who had not worked in more than a year thanks to the largesse of the taxpaying class, described to me how he spent weeks just standing around universities and other institutions carrying a protest sign. Imagine that you had entire weeks of free time, paid for by taxpayers. Would you spend this time standing around carrying a protest sign?

The next time you see a crowd gathered to protest this or that, remember that you are seeing people with a lot of time on their hands. Give a hearty salute to what is, in all probability, your tax dollars at work. The solution to this problem is obvious: Change the rules so that to bristle with the sharp quills of resentment no longer entitles one to government subsidies. Require the resentful to accept employment unless they want to starve (and employment is always there; just ask one of the millions who has sneaked across our southern border under cover of darkness.) The nightly news broadcasts would then contain far fewer scenes of the angry proletariat marching against capitalism.

In many university courses, resentment is taught not only as a virtue but, indeed, as one of the highest of virtues. In fact, in most university environments, resentment studies make up a significant portion of the curriculum. This is sometimes termed "consciousness raising" or women's studies, or black studies, but the intention is the same: to promote and exacerbate every possible kind of resentment against achievement. The aim of courses, programs, or lectures that claim to promote "awareness" or to "raise consciousness" is primarily the inculcation of resentment. If the object of such courses were to demand simple fairness for these groups—for example, equal rights to vote, to hold property, and so on—a certain amount of partisan activity would be readily defensible. No person of noble thought could possibly object to reasonable demands for equal treatment by any group: the right to pursue a trade or profession without legal hindrance or the right to simple symmetry in the law. But such is clearly no longer the case, for not only has legal symmetry and equality been achieved, it has actually been surpassed: The law now discriminates in favor of these groups. But such an unprecedented victory is still not enough: The resentful are determined to see how many further concessions might profitably be wrung from guilt-ridden achievers. Hence, they dwell upon past abuses per- petrated by persons long dead upon others who died equally long ago. Such courses seek to instill not knowledge but anger and revengefulness.

If such courses consisted simply of the objective study of history, they would be quite unobjectionable, for it is obviously not possible to study the history of a whole nation by ignoring any major part of it. For example, to study Black American culture, or Native American culture, is every bit as worthwhile and profitable as studying Italian-American culture, German-American culture, or that of any other ethnic group.

Resentment studies can be distinguished from genuine scholarship by the absence of corresponding studies and courses representing groups that have, on the whole, achieved economic success. Such a profound asymmetry is an unfailing sign of resentment, with the weaker group demanding not merely equal treatment but special privileges, and the stronger group never daring to complain lest they be thought intolerant. (Only those noble in character ever reflect on whether they are being intolerant of other groups. No Marxist or fascist swine ever lost sleep worrying about whether the group being crushed under his boot was being treated fairly. And into this tiny crack of self-doubt, resentment seeks to drive a truck. If you sometimes ask yourself whether you are being fair to persons less powerful than yourself, it is a good sign and suggests that you probably are indeed fair most of the time: But if you are constantly worrying about it, they have made you their patsy.) If there is ever any question about which of two conflicting groups in a society is benificent and which exploitative, inquire if there are any special privileges and favors granted by one group to the other, which if reversed would provoke cries of outrage from both. If the answer is yes, it indicates conclusively that the group granting the special treatment is far more tolerant, benificent, and noble than the group demanding and receiving the favoritism.

We have black studies everywhere, but the very notion of white studies sounds repugnant and racist. Yet if the motivation for black studies were genuine scholarship, there would be no reason why white studies would not be equally legitimate as a course of study. Clearly, what passes for black studies aims primarily at the cultivation and growth of resentment among blacks and guilt among whites. Any useful learning that may occur is merely incidental. The same holds true of women's studies. (Feminist resentment routinely depicts men as wicked exploiters who constantly make demands on women. Is it surprising that women who imbibe this venom feel alienated from their mates, finding it impossible to express tenderness to the "enemy?") Any attempt to institute men's studies would certainly be met with howls of protest everywhere, yet there is no reason why the symmetry should not exist—except for the component of resentment; for if there should exist any course of study in which men preached resentment against women the way women's studies teaches distrust, suspicion, and anger against men—or if whites sought to instill anti-black attitudes the way black studies instills anti-white attitudes—it would be universally denounced as an outrage.

But when such calumny originates from the corner of resentment, it generally falls within the zone of free attack against achievement—a blow not quite large enough to retaliate. Only when the blows struck by resentment step beyond mere insult and venture out into violent action does achievement decisively react. These limits were tested many times in the late 1960s and early 1970s, before the current truce and its lines of demarcation were established. Had resentment encountered total pusillanimity during its advances of 1968-72, a full-scale revolt of the lower classes would have ensued, with the likely result being the destruction of the Western economy, and probably the loss of freedom and democracy as well. Fortunately, although infected with a near-fatal dose of the poison of resentment at that time, bourgeois achievement survived and thereby acquired a pro-found—although probably temporary—distaste for the politics of extreme resentment, leading up to the conservative Reagan era a decade afterward. The Western nations stared directly into the face of what at the time passed for "liberation" and saw that it really contained nothing but tyranny, hatred, and destruc-tion. As a consequence, domestic resentment will never again successfully masquerade as "liberation" during the lifetimes of those who directly experienced the upheavals of the 1960s. It will probably happen again eventually, however, because hardly anybody ever really learns anything from history.

The graduates, and most especially the teachers, of resentment studies end up with their own personal resentments polished to an exceptionally high degree. They have learned to rationalize every difficulty faced by their group, and by themselves in particular, as being due to the malice of achievers. Such people go through life with colossal-sized chips on their shoulders. They never expect to have to compete for jobs, housing, or other goods like everyone else; when they encounter the slightest difficulty in any of these areas, they just shout "discrimination" and help comes running. They attribute every failure resulting from their own lack of striving as further proof of an evil conspiracy against them. In an achievement-oriented society, no one could make a career out of teaching resentment, just as no one could extract a living by milking other people's guilt, for ultimately only achievement can pay anyone's bills. Unfortunately, today resentment is all too often successful in convincing some achievers, through the inculcation of guilt, that resentment studies are an indispensable part of the curriculum.

My own life's experience clearly suggests to me that no one can feel truly satisfied until one is fully allied with one's inborn sense of accomplishment, with the morality of achievement. To seek satisfaction otherwise is to attempt to derive something positive from ultimately negative emotions, from destructiveness itself. To feel whole, unleash the achiever that lies within you, and say an unambiguous "NO" to every manifestation of resentment, whenever and wherever it arises. Only when we feel unashamed pride in our achievements, and confidence in our own ability to accomplish whatever may in the future be needed, do we feel fully self-realized. (Christian resentment calls this kind of self-esteem "the sin of pride," in order to better preserve your feeling of wretchedness.)

To harbor resentment of any kind not only puts one at odds with one's own economic self-interest and with the process by which civilization is maintained and advanced but also with one's own search for inner tranquility. Achievers do not worry about whether the resentful will mock their achievements, or think poorly of their failure to live up to transient standards of what is fashionable or "cool." Those who think in such ways are obviously in the thrall of some resentful ideal, a pseudo-standard whose only criterion is flamboyant perversity, and whose full realization can lead only to destruction. Such people are self-programmed for failure in life. Their opinion matters only if you intend to follow in their path.

I am convinced that most people who are filled with strong resentment of one kind or another feel very bad about themselves most of the time. How could happiness ever be possible for those who unceasingly torment themselves with their own intense envy? Their lives undoubtedly contain some periods of happiness, but the misery, the self-doubt, the wretchedness, is never far away, and clearly predominates. Christians are quite explicit about the need to feel wretched, elevating suffering and guilt to a moral duty. Socialists likewise require one to sacrifice one's own interests, one's own happiness, so that others may allegedly have more. Having done less for themselves, these others are thus seen as all the more worthy. The rulers of Marxist countries are dead-set against their subjects enjoying "decadent bourgeois pleasures." Many of the destructive acts performed by the resentful no doubt represent a desperate attempt to escape from the wretchedness they feel by striking out against those who they feel are responsible for their problems—those who have disciplined themselves to succeed. But such attempts are bound to fail. To conquer a feeling of wretchedness, one must first conquer one's resentments. Only when one sets aside the love of exhibitionistic destructivness; only when one stops savoring trite displays of petty vindictiveness and starts concentrating on the positive aspects of life—only then does one make contact with the tranquility, the feeling of nobility, that lies within us all.

So thoroughly has resentment permeated our society that

our very notions of good and bad, of right and wrong, are derived from Christian resentment. "Good" means the poor, the irresolute, the lazy, the improvident. "Bad" means the affluent, the self-disciplined, the successful, the capable. These ideas are strongly reinforced by socialist resentment. Such notions were obviously invented by life's failures to rationalize their own shortcomings. Certainly, no successful person, no capable person, no person satisfied with his own abilities could have invented such an antimorality.

I think that our notions of what is good and what is bad should derive from the accomplishments of our finest achievers, not from the resentments of our angriest failures. The forward-looking person, the person who accepts responsibility in life—the achiever—must live by a more noble set of values. To achieve. To succeed. To be truthful. To respect the lives, rights, and property of others. To assist others when he deems it appropriate—not out of a sense of guilt, but from a feeling of joyful abundance. In short, to accomplish great things in a context of noble behavior. Think of the prosperous and happy future that can be ours if we are courageous enough to exalt as our highest morality not the angry resentments of our worst failures but the splendid achievements of those responsible for our most notable, most noble successes.

5.
Resentment Against Science, Technology, and Medicine

Given that resentment is the hatred of success and strength, the powerful and widespread resentment against science, technology, and medicine that exists today should come as no surprise. No other discipline can boast of the kind of success and influence that science has enjoyed over the past few centuries. Virtually every aspect of our lives has been transformed by its seemingly relentless march. Few ideas in history have been as powerful as those of experimental science in transforming human life—and whenever something has been dramatically successful, there will be widespread resentment against it.

SCIENCE, TECHNOLOGY, AND MEDICINE

It would seem that something that lightens the load, relieves human suffering, prolongs life, and provides an endless profusion of leisure-time diversions would be universally hailed as a magnificent benefactor. Although science has occasionally raised some difficult problems, they are by no means as bad as the problems people routinely faced in prescientific times. The rise of technology has likewise not been without its problems, but the problems caused by technology are themselves susceptible to technological solutions. Any reasonably fair and impartial analysis would have to conclude that the progress of science (and its offspring—technology and medicine) has for the most part immeasurably improved our lives. But to expect that kind of reasonable analysis to prevail is to seriously overestimate the human race, for it neglects the force that repeatedly limits and reverses civilization's advances: resentment against achievement.

While it is true that many people—especially those who understand science best—view it in a highly positive light, profound resentments against science exist even among apparently educated persons. In a 1985 poll, 55 percent of Americans randomly selected believed that scientific researchers' specialized knowledge gave them a "dangerous" power.[1] People were generally willing to accept human-neutral scientific findings, such as continental drift, but they showed a great reluctance to believe in Darwinian evolution or that the brain can be understood in material terms. Thus we see that one major factor working to increase resentment against science is its success in overturning religious dogmas, especially those that accord a unique nonmaterial status and origin to the human race.

Many antiscientific resentments typically begin with the

assertion that science somehow "dehumanizes" us, as if people were more human when we were living in barbarian tribes. This argument usually ends up with some sort of restatement of the "noble savage" myth: that people were happier, freer, and more "whole" when living as savages "in harmony with nature." Here we see potent resentment in a crystalline form: the barely disguised hatred of civilization itself. The "noble savage" myth lives on most strongly among those who identify not with the achievers who build civilizations and keep them running, but with those who—cognizant of having contributed nothing to the civilization that surrounds them—secretly wish to see it destroyed because it serves as a continual reminder of their own shortcomings.

Of course real savages are not nearly so felicitous as those of popular fiction. Constantly assailed by disease, poor nutrition, parasites, and high infant mortality, the reality of primitive life was summed up nicely in Hobbes' famous phrase: "solitary, poor, nasty, brutish, and short."[2] In every instance, primitive peoples coming into contact with more developed civilizations gradually adopt most, if not all, of the inventions and conveniences of the latter. In the entire history of the world, a civilized nation with highly developed commerce, housing, and so on has never once, upon encountering a less-developed civilization, willingly abandoned its refined lifestyle for the crude life of the savage. There are, however, plenty of examples of the reverse. Thus human history is unanimous in preferring civilization over savagery. But artists, romantics, and even some philosophers sometimes beg to disagree—at least in words if not in action. (I am not aware of any among them who have actually taken their pronouncements seriously and adopted the lifestyle of a hunter/gatherer. Romantics may retire to their Walden Pond to contemplate the beauty of nature, but remember that even Thoreau made frequent trips back to Concord for companionship and supplies—it was only a mile and a half away. Thoreau admits in his journal that, for many years, whatever he could not grow himself or obtain through barter he stole from his neighbors. Life in a genuine wilderness was too tough even for Thoreau.[3])

The man best known for romanticizing the uncivilized was Jean-Jacques Rousseau (1712-1778), that wayward philosophe who so outraged Voltaire, Hume, and Diderot. He gained notoriety when he won a prestigious essay contest with an entry claiming that the human race is by nature good but becomes corrupted by civilization. Rousseau, who was in fact a very sophisticated— if largely self-taught—thinker, proclaimed himself a "simple man," and he disdained all pretensions of learning or refinement. Nonetheless, he frequented the salons of the aristocracy along with the other major literary figures of his era, all the time calling attention to himself by a bizarre and outrageous style of dress. His philosophy was a mixture of primitivism and collectivism, emphasizing that freedom consisted in the submission of the individual to the "general will." Much of nineteenth-century romanticism's spirit of hostility to science and civilization derives from Rousseau, and his influence is still strong even today.

The "noble savage" myth lives on in at least a hundred forms. In North America, most people think of the American Indian as living peacefully in glorious harmony with nature until they were "corrupted" and ultimately destroyed by an encroaching civilization. The truth, however, is not nearly so enchanting. Most Indian tribes were constantly raiding and battling each other. Many of the tribes ruthlessly exploited nature, with never a thought for tomorrow. When they had killed off the game or exhausted the soil at one location, they moved on to the next. Some Indians deliberately set the prairie on fire in order to stampede huge herds of buffalo, resulting in prodigious waste of land and animals.

Some people who view the apparent felicity and total liberty of animals imagine that humans might enjoy living in such a manner, free from all material possessions and civilized restraints. But a moment's reflection should serve to dispel that notion completely. It is typically during daylight and in pleasant weather that we see animals scurrying about. But unlike ourselves, most animals do not have heated or even truly sheltered places to hide from winter storms or furious rains. All of the animals we encounter outdoors in the pleasant afternoon are still outside throughout the freezing night, struggling to stay warm and dry. The robust and healthy among them survive, but there is no reason to view that kind of existence as desirable.

Furthermore, animals typically seem to be so young, vibrant, and healthy, that we fail to reflect upon the obvious: Old animals, and even middle-aged ones, cannot successfully compete in the difficult struggle to stay alive. We frequently see old age creeping up on domestic animals that lead pampered lives, but we never encounter old birds or arthritic squirrels in the wild. The reason is obvious: when every day is a fierce struggle for existence, the slightest decline from peak vigor virtually seals one's fate. Civilization may be viewed essentially as a scheme for bending (although not breaking) this iron law—for debrutalizing nature to some extent in order to increase the degree of dysfunction that it is possible to suffer and yet still live. With civilization, we seek to delay death as long as absolutely possible.

In spite of all rational arguments to the contrary, many people still perceive civilization as a blight against nature instead of the life-enhancing force it really is. This is yet another of the unfortunate legacies we inherited from the Age of Romanticism—that heroic but ultimately irrational rebellion against the mind's achievements. Economic growth itself is perceived as some kind of sin against nature, and in any confrontation between ecology and technology, the environmentalists are automatically presumed to be in the right. I am not arguing that the landscape should be cavalierly destroyed, but any thinking person surely recognizes that there must be a rational tradeoff between economic growth and nature, or else we should all still be living in caves. Resentment, however, sees all profit-making activity as wrong, and especially so when achievement wishes to develop some pretty, natural spot "merely" to create houses and jobs.

When people see abundant new housing being built, they often call it "urban sprawl." (But when housing is in short supply, they demand that the government "do something" about it.) When people see new stores and factories being built, indicating vigorous economic growth, this is called "blight." (Where I live and work are called "home" and "work," respectively. Where you live and work are called "sprawl" and "blight.") I am not denying that much new construction reflects appallingly bad taste, and that much of it does make me want to take the back of my hand and knock it from the landscape, but that is an aesthetic and architectural problem, not an economic one. We must remember that in a free society, the greatest profit is to be made by satisfying the needs of the many, not of the few, since the middle class controls by far the greatest portion of the national income. And if the many happen to have dismal taste, then they shall be punished by having to live in shoe-box housing. With the explosion in housing costs in recent decades, owing in large part to "no-growth" restrictions on construction, a novel dilemma has arisen: Educated persons of refined tastes seeking aesthetically pleasant surroundings are now frequently compelled to live in neighborhoods that had been constructed cheaply and hastily thirty years earlier as mass housing for the aesthetically blind lower-middle classes. But they shouldn't complain too loudly. The lower economic growth rates have caused the children of the original owners of those houses to be priced out of the housing market altogether, forcing them into small apartments or else into lower-cost towns far away.

In recent years, the "environmental movement" has become so dominated by resentment against prosperity that its original goal of stopping pollution seems to have not only gotten lost, but in many instances actually inverted. Nobody, myself included, wants to see the air become polluted or bodies of water become toxic. To genuinely appreciate the natural world in all its splendor is an expression of the highest taste. There is great wisdom in the natural world. It is a finely tuned system of natural harmonies—of rocks sculptured by obeying the laws of physics for millions of years, of creatures finely honed by eons of Darwinian selection. When people we once called "conservationists" sought to preserve some of the finest examples of our planet's beauty from irreversible—and in many cases totally unneces-sary—destruction, it was an effort that every sensitive person could easily support.

Today, however, "environmentalism" is typically nothing more than a large-caliber weapon in the politics of resentment. It is merely a fig leaf to hide the ugliness of resentment against science, against technology, against economic growth (which always brings sinful profit to someone), and especially against civilization itself. "Environmentalists" automatically oppose the construction of new roads, of major buildings and shopping centers, of airports, of mines, and most vehemently of all, of facilities for the production and distribution of energy—especially if they are nuclear. It does not matter whether the proposed development is ecologically and/or economically sound. All such developments are to be stopped wherever possible, using any suitable pretext whatever. If it cannot be stopped, it is to be delayed as long as possible in the hopes that future developments will be stifled by the exploding costs of interest on construction capital during the years of politically induced delay.

Nowhere is this more clearly seen than in the antinuclear movement. Nuclear power is the safest, cleanest, most benign form of energy production yet devised. Its wastes, which are small in volume, can be sealed in canisters and placed in deep, geologically stable strata, thus preventing them from interacting with the biosphere. On the other hand, the burning of coal or other fossil fuels, which are the only viable large-scale alter-natives, discharges wastes directly into the atmosphere, where they end up in peoples' lungs. One would think that any true environmentalist would encourage the use of nuclear power, as did the Sierra Club before it was radicalized in the late 1960s.[4]

No member of the public outside the Soviet bloc has yet been killed or even injured in a nuclear power accident—a statement which cannot be made about any other form of energy production. The Soviet nuclear accident at Chernobyl proves only that the Soviets are incapable of building a safe reactor, not that a safe reactor cannot be built. The Soviets are likewise incapable of building automobiles, cameras, video recorders, TV sets, or computers reliable enough to sell in world markets, but nobody suggests that these things are impossible to build. In any case, the Chernobyl reactor was built to maximize power output, not safety, and it had no containment building "in case of an accident." Yet despite its irresponsible design and operation, to date fewer than a hundred people have died in this "worst case" accident, a toll frequently exceeded in coal mine disasters. In the United States, the accident at Three Mile Island conclusively demonstrated the safety of American power reactors. In spite of gross errors of operation that caused the reactor to go totally out of control, nobody was killed or injured, and the amount of radiation leaked into the environment was utterly negligible, scare-mongering stories notwithstanding.

So why do the forces of resentment so vehemently oppose nuclear power? Because some people are infuriated by the sight of any economic growth in which they personally do not share (even if it is because they never tried offering value for value). They are infuriated by the sight of someone—anyone—getting rich. Wanting to stop or reverse economic development, they could not hope to find a more effective way of doing this than by preventing the application of the most promising new technologies.

Hence the insane opposition to safe, clean, and cheap nuclear energy. Hence the mad Luddite opposition to applications of genetic engineering, one of the most promising new technologies ever for extending and improving human life. In a few short years, genetic engineering has already given us drugs that prolong the lives of diabetics and heart attack patients, and it promises countless other medical benefits in the years to come. However, the resentful oppose it vehemently because they know all this progress will make some capitalist rich. (Imagine the battles to be fought when molecular assembler technology becomes a reality!)

Even today's well-established economic mainstay, the automobile, encounters visceral opposition in certain circles that seek to force everyone onto government-controlled "mass transit." Imagine the economic cost if it were possible to roll back the use of electricity itself. Yet the contrived "energy shortages," caused by government price controls and socialist-model allocation schemes were a first step down this dismal path, a path we have fortunately turned away from, at least for now.

Can it be that resentment really does vehemently oppose the most promising new technologies, seeking to stifle economic growth? Whether by connivance or by an instinct refined by a lifetime of practice, their anger is directed precisely at those areas showing the greatest potential for economic growth, like a deer nibbling on the newest, tenderest green shoots. If you are still not convinced, reflect on those things that resentment is working the hardest to undermine. It is not just nuclear energy and genetic engineering. Resentment has also created a significant amount of hysteria aimed at slowing down or stopping the growth of computers in the workplace by claiming that video display terminals are health hazards. Imagine the economic damage to be done if scientifically illiterate workers could be frightened away from their computer terminals. After looking into these wild claims, the American Medical Association found absolutely nothing to substantiate the alleged health hazards of VDTs (confirming many other scientific studies), yet the hysterical claims continue.[5] These same people who fear they may be done in by a computer monitor nonetheless think nothing of going home to stare for hours at TV sets, which may emit far more low-level radiation than any VDT. But resentment is under no obligation to be rational.

Similar hysteria has been raised about the alleged safety hazards of chemicals used in the manufacture of electronic integrated circuits. Think of the economic harm to be done if workers could be frightened out of the "clean rooms" where integrated circuits are produced. While these and other chemicals can, of course, be harmful when improperly handled or used, many, if not most, claims of harm resulting from their use are, at best, medically questionable and appear to go far beyond what can be convincingly demonstrated to skeptical physicians. Similarly, colossal waves of shrill hysteria have been raised in the Silicon Valley and elsewhere about alleged chemical contamination of the groundwater resulting from high-tech companies. Think of the brake on economic growth if communities could be scared into refusing to allow such plants to operate. But state-of-the-art measuring techniques now allow us to detect minute quantities of contaminants that are orders of magnitude below levels that have any effect. This creates opportunity for hyperbole and hysteria in instances where absolutely no harm has come to anyone, transforming an early warning of a possible future problem into a pretended life-threatening catastrophe.

The degree of popular resentment against the esoteric and powerful knowledge of science, technology, and medicine explains the strong appeal of pseudoscience, which teaches that all of the educated people of the world are completely off-base, and that simple-minded answers are the most profound. Pseudoscientists claim that science is missing out on the greatest discoveries of all. They believe in such things as alien visitors, monsters living in our lakes and forests, and that dreaded diseases can be cured by simple folk remedies. But first we are supposed to turn away from intellectual answers and embrace simple-minded ones. Pseudoscience attempts to assert the superiority of the uneducated, and the victory of proud ignorance over learning and accomplishment.

Pseudoscience is the manifestation of the belief that ignorant answers are better than carefully reasoned ones, that the haphazard belief systems of the common people are more correct than those of the scientific and technical elite. The pseudosciences delight the resentful by portraying sages as simpletons and simpletons as sages, just as Marxism delights the unproductive with its inversion of capitalism's notions of good and bad. Consequently, the overall level of belief in the pseudosciences tends to rise and fall with the ebb and flow of resentment in society at large, no matter what form that resentment may take. The belief in miracles increased dramatically as Christianity, which represented powerful resentments against the secular knowledge of the philosophers, advanced throughout the Roman world. Similarly, the pseudosciences surged boldly forward in the 1960s, riding on the coattails of the socialist resentment which was then triumphant in politics.

It slowly ebbed in the late 1970s and early 1980s as the once-shining promises of the radical Left dissolved into the realities of inflation, recession, the Vietnamese Gulag, and the Cambodian killing fields. Former student radicals of the 1960s turned their efforts to the pursuit of achievement in their careers, no longer enthralled by simplistic, resentful portrayals of establishment scientists as closed-minded dolts.

A psychology similar to that of pseudoscience underlies fundamentalism in all religions, whether Christian, Moslem, or other. Fundamentalists are profoundly resentful of those people whose knowledge is real, whose claim to wisdom does not rest on the authority of dubious "revelations," whose knowledge can profitably be applied in the real world. Religious fundamentalism asserts the superiority of dogmatic ignorance over secular learning. It is the assault of angry ignorance against hard-earned wisdom. It should not be surprising that religious fundamentalists are sometimes severe critics of pseudoscientific beliefs: They are competitors, like bacteria and mold, both attempting to occupy the same psychological niche.

Fundamental to all forms of resentment is the rejection of the discipline implicit in achievement. Nowhere is this more easily seen than in the rejection of the strict mental discipline that is the hallmark of science, technology, mathematics, and medicine; for pseudoscience relies on "intuition," and religious fundamentalism on "faith."

No worthwhile achievement is ever attained without discipline. Whether we look at the requirements to become a successful surgeon or a manager of a business or even a first-rate plumber, we see that in every case it requires specialized knowledge, experience in utilizing that knowledge, and careful attention to detail. While some disciplines are more difficult to master than others, every occupation requires that some skill be mastered to do the job well. In many cases, this knowledge and experience does not come easily, and this is especially true in technical fields in which years of college-level study are requisite for attaining even the most minimal level of competency. Resentment, however, cannot bear to think that the competent have in some way earned their rewards, for that would undermine the whole edifice of resentment-morality, which teaches that the poor are worthy, and the rich are sinful.

Therefore, it is necessary to invent pseudosciences, which can be mastered by any fool spouting a few mystical words. This new-found pseudoknowledge enables those who are uneducated and/or resentful to surpass, at least in their own minds, the knowledge and power of those who have invested years in rigorous scientific discipline. Doctors may be unable to cure advanced cancers, but the charismatic faith healer pretends he can, calling on Jesus, and often telling sufferers to stop taking their prescribed medications. "Doctors don't know nearly as much as those self-taught Baptist preachers," the resentful tell each other. "They don't need no fancy science—they heal with the word of God." Of course, anyone who rigorously followed up on those allegedly "healed" by such flimflam would find that they fare no better than people suffering from the same condition who do not go to faith healers. James Randi, a magician known as "The Amazing Randi," recently investigated many of today's leading faith healers, and found that many of them practice deception and chicanery. Ten years before Randi, the late Dr. William Nolen made similar investigations into faith healing, with similar results.[6] But carefully investigating claims of this kind takes considerable effort and discipline. Since disciplined investigation is not an activity undertaken by the resentful, such claims, at least for them, go unchallenged, and the results of others' skeptical investigations, if known, are not believed for the same reasons that caused them to doubt the consensus of medical science in the first place.

With claims of "psychic powers," such as predicting the future, clairvoyantly receiving information, or psychically affecting physical objects, the deceitful or the self-deluded are able to surpass, at least in the eyes of the credulous, the magnificent achievements of physicists, astronomers, and other scientists who have painstakingly unlocked many of the mysteries of the universe. Of course, such claims never stand up to critical scrutiny; the pages of the *Skeptical Inquirer* are filled with carefully researched criticisms of psychic claims, and not one such claim has ever been substantiated to the satisfaction of the scientific community at large.[7] However, at the risk of being repetitive, let me restate that critical scrutiny requires discipline and hence is a trait found among achievers, not the resentful.

A belief in "psychic powers" allows one to believe that anyone may at any time achieve far greater knowledge and mastery of the universe than a whole conclave of Nobel laureates in physics, and that they can reach that state without having undertaken any disciplined study whatsoever. A housewife who dropped out of high school and who has never held a steady job in her life will be revered as a great sage if she can convince the credulous that she is blessed with "psychic powers." Indeed, wide-eyed reporters will compose wholly uncritical and flattering stories about her alleged abilities, almost never calling them into question. She can demand and get hourly fees from a multitude of clients (there's one born every minute) that far exceed those earned by doctors and architects who have invested years of sweat and toil in building their careers.

To claim success in creating an alleged "perpetual motion" device allows one to become an instant Galileo, for the claim carries with it a pre-arranged rejection by the Patent Office, conferring automatic martyrdom. Regardless of whether the supposed inventor is deceitful or merely deluded, the inventor can pose as having accomplished a task so difficult that not only have the greatest scientists of the past and the present failed where he has succeeded, but they have even pronounced the task to be impossible. Often the inventor appeals strongly to provincialism. Of course, the machine can never be carefully examined by skeptics, since it always fails to work when test conditions are too stringent. However, it serves its purpose by allowing the resentful to imagine a humble, home-grown crank to be on a par with the greatest physicist, if only for a short time.

People at the bottom of the economic ladder hardly ever profess to believe that those near the top arrived there through skill, education, hard work, and a willingness to take risks. (Many of them no doubt realize this but are unwilling to express it openly.) If they were to acknowledge this, they would be forced to blame their dismal state on their own shortcomings, which is psychologically unacceptable. Therefore, the lower classes imagine that the people at the top have either stolen their money or else simply have better "luck." Consequently, we find an entire industry devoted to the cultivation of "luck," which to judge from its advertising, is flourishing. Everyone knows that mass-circulation tabloid newspapers and magazines dazzle their readers with exciting—although highly questionable—accounts of pseudoscientific miracles. Less well known is the fact that these publications, which do not exactly cater to the affluent, are literally filled with ads for dozens of different "lucky charms," each containing an exotic story to suggest great potency. The ad may offer you a candle, an amulet, or a necklace. Its powers may derive from a Gypsy fortune teller's spell, or the waters at Lourdes, or perhaps from a mysterious stranger who came from nowhere and vanished into the night, never to be seen again. In each case, the "lucky charm" promises to bring health, happiness, prosperity, an end to marital discord, or just generally fix whatever may be troubling you. No action of any kind is required on your part (except writing a check). You need not change any bad habits, learn any new skills, or learn how to manage your money more wisely. All the problems of your life are supposedly due to "bad luck," and the magic trinket is supposed to change your "luck."

Similarly, faith healers and evangelists who minister primarily to the profoundly unsophisticated routinely send out "blessed" trinkets, which may be pieces of cloth or samples of "holy oil" in a tiny plastic package. They stress that God will change your "luck" and bring you a financial blessing, provided that you send money to the evangelist.

These examples clearly reveal a magical world-view that unfortunately is alive and well today. It is the prescientific outlook of the savage. It is difficult to see how anyone could hold such beliefs today when so much is known about how the universe works. However, this knowledge is strongly concentrated in the hands of a technological elite and is not equitably distributed. (Perhaps there must be a sinister conspiracy keeping knowledge of science from the proletariat? I'm joking, of course: most proletarian youth will heatedly defy or possibly even assault anyone who tries to teach them the mental discipline of science.) The weekly tabloid papers sold in supermarkets, in which the magical world-view is exploited, have circulations far higher than that of any respectable news daily or weekly, proving that gross ignorance and abject credulity are not exactly rare.

Those who hold such childish beliefs about the way the universe works insist that they should make as much money as others, since they imagine that differences in income level are due primarily to "luck." They become very envious of the affluent, since they are unable to understand how a belief in magic prevents anyone from setting and achieving realistic plans and goals. Worse yet, most church leaders—and more than a few politicians—share this anger of the unproductive. Of course, a moment's reflection should make it obvious that any person who believes that affluence is caused by luck must necessarily be poor.

One often finds a considerable degree of resentment against science in artistic circles and in the humanities. This is a consequence of learning's separation into "two cultures" that seldom understand each other: the hard sciences and the humanities, a distinction made fashionable by C. P. Snow. Typically, successful college graduates in science and engineering are eagerly recruited by corporate employers, and offered high salaries. But the opposite is true in the arts and humanities. In those disciplines, graduates must compete frantically to get any job at all in their chosen field, no matter how low-paying or unattractive. In the end many of them are forced to leave their fields completely and take unrelated jobs, such as in retail sales or restaurants. It is thus not surprising at all that some of these people might feel considerable resentment against the influence and financial success of those in the sciences, as well as against the capitalist economic system itself, which they hold responsible for their own poverty and powerlessness.

But when we look at the situation from an economic point of view, the reason things work out as they do is perfectly obvious. Because many talented people find working in the arts and humanities to be attractive and they are qualified to perform this work, it is not at all difficult to find people who are willing and able to fill the few such positions that open up each year. Consequently it is not necessary to pay large salaries to attract and retain these people. (Many people forget that any job's salary is, of course, nothing but a measure of how difficult it is to attract and hold someone competent to perform the given task.) In technical fields, however, the large demand owing to the great economic utility of technical expertise ensures that qualified persons, who make up a relatively small percentage of the population, will be in short supply, thereby driving up the price. Furthermore, there are at least some people who, while they care little for computers or engineering, are in those fields primarily because there is good money to be made. But nobody becomes an art teacher or a historian in order to get a fat salary.

Resentment against science is fueled by the anger that inevitably builds up against members of a successful elite, even when the members of the elite must first earn their positions by difficult study and careful research. This resentment persists in spite of the fact that the elite have contributed greatly to the health, living standard, and longevity of the entire population. Given that the technological elite are both prosperous and powerful, things could be no other way. This resentment is exacerbated by the degree of self-discipline required for the understanding of science, which utterly rules out membership in this club for the undisciplined, the confused, and the profoundly resentful. The very obscurity of scientific knowledge to outsiders infuriates the resentful, causing them to invent counterfeit, pseudoscientific solutions which any fool can understand. Of course, if the universe chose to arrange itself in ways that are not instantly comprehensible to the mentally undisciplined, it is not the fault of those who have been able to fathom its intricacies. More emphasis on science education in the schools would no doubt help alleviate this problem somewhat.

"How dare these people know things that others don't, things which give them a dangerous power?" ask the resentful. "How dare they know things not immediately accessible to others? It isn't fair." Hence, pseudosciences are invented to address this perceived injustice, raising every crank to the stature of a Galileo and lowering every scientist to that of a blockhead too blind and stupid to see what is obvious to the illiterate. This enables the profoundly resentful to evade the painful reality that understanding how the universe works requires diligence, patience, disciplined effort, and competence—qualities that in the resentful are generally lacking. The resentful do not understand that the universe does not make concessions to ignorance. The natural laws of the universe are what they are, regardless of who does or does not like them. The universe itself discriminates against the stupid and the foolhardy; it takes no pity on anyone. It grants no second chances for incompetence; it allows no exceptions to its ironclad rules on the grounds of ignorance.

Resentment confuses the inflexible laws of the universe with the squishy-soft laws made and sporadically enforced by tolerant achievement, which fears the appearance of being intolerant more than it fears anything else. Hence achievement is forever softening its laws as it becomes apparent that there are many who can not or will not comply with them. Unsophisticated resentment expects to find the same forgiveness in nature's laws. Consequently, those who simmer with resentment against the inflexibility of the laws of the universe—laws that seem to unfairly single out the inept for special punishment—project that anger upon those who thrive under the very same rules. Surely it must be luck that some people do not have so many accidents, or do not suffer so many setbacks and tragedies. (Or might it actually be a better understanding of how to live and prosper under nature's laws?) However, no amount of seething resentment will change the laws of the universe one bit or give the slightest validity to the infantile pseudosciences that have been invented by the resentful to assuage their own feelings of impotent revengefulness.

NOTES

1. "Poll Finds Distrust of Science," story by Deborah Blum, *Sacramento Bee.* The poll was taken by Jon Miller of Northern Illinois University, and was reported at the 1987 meeting of the American Association for the Advancement of Science. From the *San Jose Mercury News,* Feb. 24, 1987.

2. Hobbes, *Leviathan,* part 1, chapter 1.

3. Thoreau, journal entry dated January 3, 1861: "It is true that we as yet take liberties and go across lots, and steal, or 'hook,' a good many things, but we naturally take fewer and fewer liberties every year, as we meet with more resistance." Many people have called Thoreau a libertarian, but to me he typifies the achievement-hating, theft-oriented values of unproductive people.

4. As antidotes to resentment's misrepresentations of the risks of nuclear energy, see: Beckmann, Peter, *The Health Hazards of Not Going Nuclear* (Boulder, Co.: Golem Press, 1976); Hoffman, P. L., ed., *The Technology of High-Level Nuclear Waste Disposal (Springfield, Va.: National Technical Information Center, 1984); Health Effects of Low-level Radiation* (American Council on Science and Health, 1988).

5. "Health Effects of Video Display Terminals," Council on Scientific Affairs, *Journal of the American Medical Association,* March 20, 1987.

6. Randi, James, *The Faith Healers* (Buffalo, N.Y.: Prometheus Books, 1988); Nolen, William A., M.D., *Healing: A Doctor in Search of a Miracle* (New York: Random House, 1974).

7. The *Skeptical Inquirer,* a quarterly publication of the Committee for the Scientific Investigation of Claims of the Paranormal, Box 229, Central Park Station, Buffalo, NY, 14125.

6.
The Arts

The values of a given group of people or social class are reflected in the art or would-be art that they admire. All peoples in all places throughout history have some form of music, some form of literature (either written or oral), and some kind of drama and poetry that is uniquely theirs. And in these arts, we can see a reflection of the values held by the people who patronize them; for all art attempts to provide answers, consciously or otherwise, to such fundamental questions as "What is man?" and "What is it that matters in life?"

For the great majority of people the only arts are the popular arts. This has always been the case. However, the form the popular arts take changes radically with time. At many times in the past, major elements of the popular arts were derived, at least in part, from the fine arts. Consider, for example, the many operettas written by such composers as Victor Herbert and Rudolf Friml, which were so popular in Europe and America around 1900. The debt these forms of popular entertainment owe to the grand opera of the period is obvious.

As soon as movies acquired a soundtrack, they were filled with the music of popular singers like Alan Jones, Jeanette Macdonald, Nelson Eddy, and others whose singing styles were clearly influenced by opera. Some celebrated opera singers, such as Lauritz Melchior and Lilly Pons, actually became film stars. (Melchior's very large footprints can be seen set in concrete outside Hollywood's famous "Chinese Theater," near those of Dean Martin and Groucho Marx.) Even as recently as the 1940s and '50s, entertainer Spike Jones achieved enormous popularity with his parodies of classical music. *Operatic singing* (which is to say, singing as a rigorous discipline) and even elaborate parodies of it have all but disappeared from popular entertainment today.

Throughout most of history, orators, and especially singers, spent years practicing and perfecting their vocal techniques. They took lessons; they practiced; they were coached in the techniques of vocal perfection: enunciation, resonance, support, crystalline clarity of tone—all pursued as an exquisite art form. They pursued these techniques practicing self-mastery and discipline, as dedicated to their regimen of training as the finest athlete.

Then, in the 1920s, the development of electronic amplification techniques allowed almost anyone to pretend to be a "singer," because it was no longer necessary to develop or possess vocal technique. Electronic amplification made it possible for an untrained voice to superficially sound loud and clear, which made vocal training largely unnecessary. Anyone could now pretend to be a singer, thumbing his or her nose at self-discipline, at practice, at the very paradigm of achievement itself. Even highly amplified, an untrained voice possesses none of the dynamics or control of a classical singer, but fans of popular music no longer seemed to care. Hence, we heard at first the "crooners," whose style progressed (or rather, regressed) into soft throaty-toned popular entertainment and finally into rock's angry shouts, which are actually little more than primal screams. Of course, without a microphone stuck well into his throat, the pop music "emperor" would have no clothes. The next time you see a concert, notice that while popular singers always need microphones, classical singers scorn them. Thus electronic amplification is a crutch that has made possible the proletarization of music, allowing any undisciplined person to masquerade as a musical hero and opening up careers in singing to those who reject the very idea of vocal discipline and perhaps every other discipline as well. In fact, that particularly crude type of rock music known as "punk rock" was explicitly founded on the notion that anyone should be able to become a rock performer, regardless of talent or the lack thereof. The rejection of discipline in popular music had become complete.

Singing is not the only art form in which standards have been dramatically relaxed in recent decades. The very same phenomenon has occurred in the art of dance, as classical ballet devolves into "modern dance." The most immediately recognizable difference between the two is that modern dancers have relaxed the requirement that the ballerina be *en pointe—*

that graceful yet exceedingly difficult mode of dancing literally on the tips of one's toes. This is not what is commonly called "standing on tiptoes": the ball of the ballerina's foot does not touch the floor. She must wear a special hardened shoe to accomplish this, yet it still requires years of exercise and practice to master. Modern dancers do not even attempt this: they dance barefoot. There is also far less emphasis in modern dance on the extreme stretching of the limbs that ballerinas must master. In spite of all this, the overall repudiation of standards in dance is far less pronounced than in singing, as at least some moderately rigorous requirements are still retained. Perhaps this is because there is as yet no way for a dancer's body movements to be electronically amplified, as can be done with singing.

Today, much of the music that reaches a mass audience can be called slum rock—that music which expresses the values held by those at the absolute bottom of the socio-economic ladder. Such music must necessarily be loud—preferably loud enough to anger and shock anyone nearby who may be so unfortunate as to have even a minuscule residuum of good taste. It must also be loud enough to drown out all attempts at conversation, intelligent or otherwise, at parties and dances. I am not talking about innocuous little popular songs or tepid ballads. I am talking about the throbbing, pulsating, screaming, pounding noises that so powerfully excite the resentful, from which today there seems no escape. To appear credible, the rock performer must look utterly slovenly and should act in as rude and sullen a manner as possible; for he has an important message to convey—he must literally shout his resentment against civilization and its achievers so loudly that no one can fail to get the message.

ROBERT SHEAFFER

Rock music provides a nearly ideal vehicle for the expression of resentment, which probably explains its virtually universal popularity among the two most resentful groups in society: teenagers and slum dwellers. Both feel generally powerless and wish to deliver a potent message expressing their resentment against those who are more successful, who have far more money, and hence wield far more power: today, that means la bourgeoisie. Hence the provocatively loud, raucous music, the careful culti-vation of a wretched appearance, and the acceptance and even glorification of violence—all enhanced, of course, by the crudest possible lyrics. Much of rock music glorifies proletarian val-ues like arbitrary violence, noise, lack of discipline, uncontrolled use of drugs, and above all, hatred of the ability, intelligence, and self-discipline that makes achievement possible. Profoundly anti-intellectual in character, slum rock is the musical expression of the class war, the assault of angry ignorance against refined competence. No person with any residuum of good taste who is involuntarily exposed to such noise pollution (as we all are today nearly everywhere we go, even in our homes and in mass-audience TV shows) could fail to feel revolted. No doubt many readers have themselves discovered that complaining to some thoughtless scoundrel who is filling the world with such noise results in that person being clearly delighted to see that he has succeeded in offending someone.

Please do not make the mistake of thinking that I am opposed to or offended by sensuality in art or music. Far from it. Many of the world's greatest artistic masterpieces are explicitly sensual, and only those seriously infected by the life-pollution of asceticism find such things of beauty offensive. Consider, for example, the bawdy language in many of Shakespeare's plays, most notably *Romeo and Juliet;* the nudity of magnificent statues of the gods, which seemed natural to the Greeks; or the flagrant sensuality of Wagner's *Tristan und Isolde.* In that pair's famous love duet in Act Two, Wagner slowly builds up musical passion to climax in what is unmistakably the orchestration of the lovers' pelvic thrusts and Isolde's ecstatic screams, which are all quickly terminated by a terrifying musical *coitus interruptus.* The crucial difference is that geniuses like Shakespeare and Wagner produced masterpieces, works that testified to the supreme self-mastery and accomplishment of their creators, while rock singers produce trash. A masterpiece is still performed, studied, and revered centuries after it is written, while what passes for a great work of slum rock is all but forgotten the following year. Even the popular music of the 1920s, 1930s, and 1940s had far more staying power and thus, arguably, far more merit than the much more angry and confrontational popular music of today. Those few rock songs that have retained their popularity for twenty or thirty years—certain ones by Elvis Presley or The Beatles, for example—tend to be those that are joyful and melodic rather than loud and confrontational.

That quintessential proletarian value, arbitrary violence, is a vital element of the contemporary rock music scene. Performers often include simulated acts of gratuitous violence in their concerts or rock videos. Dolls' heads may be cut off, fake blood poured over the stage, or some other destructive act performed to screams of delight from the audience. Many rock heroes have more than once been personally involved in violent altercations. The crowd is unmistakably getting this violent message. Many times rock concert fans, after they have received a powerful dose of high-decibel hatred of achievement, turn into violent mobs. While the riot is underway, resentment gains a temporary victory over civilization; we experience a small and short-lived proletarian state.

If you disagree that hard-core rock music is fueled almost entirely by resentment, then please explain why its fans so delight in gratuitous violence. No angry mob has ever surged out of a performance by Lawrence Welk or Liberace to wreak havoc on a town. (Music is the expression of a philosophy, which while seldom put into words, is nonetheless felt by the listener. The music we like has an underlying philosophy that is agreeable to us.) There is no possible motivation or justification for such violence, and it does not benefit the mob in any direct way except one: It provides an outlet for their impotent, seething rage against the civilization that millions of achievers have built around them not only without their help but in spite of their surly opposition.

For today's youth who chooses to conform to the dictates of his peers (and pitifully few do not), rock singers are powerful role models and the realization of every resentful ideal. Consider what happens to those youth who succeed in realizing these ideals. What kind of achievements will their lives contain? What marketable skills can they acquire without compromising those ideals? If you were an employer, and someone who dressed, acted, and talked exactly like a rock singer came in to apply for a job, would you consider hiring such a person, assuming you had any choice? Could you convince yourself that such a person wishes to make a profit for you and a career for himself?

Of course not. Such people have clearly job-proofed themselves by their obvious and visible rejection of discipline and achievement, by their powerful will to poverty. They will spend the rest of their lives blaming successful achievers for the mess their lives are in.

While a civilization is in ascendance (which is to say, when the morality of achievement has the upper hand), people tend to derive their cultural and social ideals from the class above them. Something is lost, of course, in the translation, but people clearly see the class above them as an example to be imitated to the degree possible. Stated simply, the upper classes expand downward. But if and when resentment-morality gains the upper hand, civilization enters a slow decline, and people begin to see the classes below them as examples to be followed. Then, lower-class values begin to spread upward. We have unmistakably seen such a transition in the popular arts in the mid-twentieth century.

The upper classes, as well as the haute-bourgeoisie, have always opted for the fine arts, with its refined and uplifting character. However, the most striking thing about the fine arts in the twentieth century is their almost total absence. I do not mean to say that appreciation of the arts is not there. It is obviously alive and well among the educated classes. Recordings of classical music are selling briskly; not as voluminously as proletarian rock, to be sure, but educated taste always has been (and always will be) in the minority. Tickets to major productions of opera and ballet are notoriously hard to get. Art galleries containing centuries-old masterpieces are crowded with appreciative visitors.

124

Yet relatively little of great artistic merit has been produced in our twentieth century. When we compare our century to the one that preceded it, which was dominated by such titans as Beethoven, Goethe, Wagner, Renoir, Verdi, Tschaikovsky, Brahms, Dostoevski, and so on, one cannot help but weep that such explosions of creative talent have existed until comparatively recent times and now seem to have been all but extinguished. Emerson wrote of the joy he experienced as a youth when he discovered that a schoolmate of his had written uplifting verses. Recalling the incident as an adult, Emerson reflected, "It is much to know that poetry has been written this very day, under this very roof, by your side. What! that wonderful spirit has not expired! These stony moments are still sparkling and animated!"[1] Were Emerson alive today, he would be forced to conclude that this "wonderful spirit" is all but dead; that these moments remain stony.

As the most obvious example, take music. If we exclude those musical giants born during the nineteenth century whose lifetimes stretched well into the twentieth century—Giacomo Puccini, Richard Strauss, Serge Prokofiev, and even Igor Stravinski—what of enduring value remains of twentieth-century music? A few nice pieces and pleasant tunes, all but lost in a sea of garbage. Now some composers give us meaningless strings of random notes, or works to be conducted telepathically (Stockhausen), or even four minutes and thirty-three seconds of silence in three movements (Cage). Why is such buffoonery taken seriously by anyone?

Since about the time of the French Revolution, a major recurring theme running through artistic circles has been *épater la bourgeoisie,* "to shock the middle class." In *The Painted Word,* Tom Wolfe illustrates how this principle underlies the primary thrust of modern painting. Wolfe describes in his inimitably humorous style how any would-be art connoisseur who failed to see the merit of some new and totally shocking work was accused by avant-gardists of secretly harboring bourgeois tendencies, which of course made him an outcast. It would seem that a work fails to meet the standards of contemporary artists if it fails to shock those who shoulder the burden of economic responsibility. Is this not one of the most visible manifestations of resentment—to take great joy in shocking those who are in no position to be as irresponsible as you? Why did Jackson Pollock, hailed by *Life* magazine as possibly "the greatest living painter in the United States," take off all his clothes at a society party in New York City and urinate in the fireplace?[2] Did da Vinci or Rembrandt ever do that? In an era when proletarian resentment passes for higher morality, should it be so surprising to find that expressions of resentment also pass for art? And, consequently, that great art is virtually nonexistent?

All great art is ennobling, and our age is at war with the concept of human inequality. Even if a contemporary composer should write a fanfare in the grand old style, it must be written for the "common man." Of course, the common man does not want or need a glorious fanfare and probably never has; give him a mangy looking slob screaming crudely into a microphone, and he thinks it's great music. Does listening to the music of Beethoven make one feel like "the common man," i.e., resentful and self-barred from great achievement, or does it make one instead feel heroic (as in *Eroica*), the master of great thoughts and deeds? Does the music of Bach make one feel like the common man, one defeated by one's own inertia, or like a king bedecked in baroque splendor? As for Shakespeare, just listening to the language used by his characters makes one feel uplifted to a region that few ever reach. Even servants and slaves in Shakespeare muse about the meaning of man's existence in casual conversation. If these are servants, they are absurdly educated, even aristocratic.

None of these great works was written for the common man, nor has great art ever been fundamentally based in lower-class culture, although in some vital civilizations appreciation for great art has penetrated surprisingly far down from the top. Historically, great art has been supported and appreciated by the upper classes, whether the people on top arrived there passively through descent, or actively through accomplishment. In an age when no thought of human inequality may be publicly expressed without engendering violent objection, it should not be surprising that one of the most dramatic manifestations of human inequality—the ability to experience *and then convey to others* in a compelling manner truly sublime emotions and thoughts—has all but vanished.

Here is the reason that great art is gone: In order to write great music or literature or to make an enduring painting or sculpture, it is necessary to make the listener, reader, or viewer feel noble and elevated above commonplace feelings, concerns, pettiness, and ugliness. One must seek to express a delicate, evanescent idea that is valid not only for the present but for all time; one must seek a subtlety which not everyone can comprehend. This violates everything the modern artist has been

127

taught to stand for—which is to vehemently crave to see everyone brought down to a common level. Any artist who might fail to conform and attempt to produce uplifting works would be considered a traitor to the people—a lackey of the moneyed classes. In the past, an artist was expected to spend years studying, practicing, and learning to achieve. Today, many artists merely slosh paint around to express some childish level of emotion. There is little danger that future generations will mistake anything of this kind for great art.

We will better understand the interrelationship between art and politics in the last century and a half by looking at the career of the man who is unquestionably the most influential artist of the period: Richard Wagner. In *Aspects of Wagner,* Bryan Magee documents this influence, discussing those who were profoundly and directly influenced by Wagner.[3] The list includes James Joyce, T. S. Eliot, Nietzsche, Baudelaire, Zola, Proust, Cézanne, Renoir, Gauguin, Debussy, Massenet, Bruckner, Mahler, Strauss, Holst, Bartók, Thomas Mann, George Bernard Shaw, Virginia Woolf, D. H. Lawrence, W. H. Auden— and many others (to which we must add H. L. Mencken), which is to say, practically every creative artist who mattered during the late nineteenth and early twentieth centuries.

In 1834, the young revolutionary Richard Wagner risked prison by loudly singing the *Marseillaise* from his hotel balcony in Teplitz in Bohemia, urging people in the street to join him in defiance of the police. His participation in the abortive revolution of 1848, while he was conductor of the Dresden Opera, caused him to flee to Switzerland to avoid arrest. While in Switzerland he became active in German exile circles and began work on his extraordinarily ambitious *Ring des Nibelungen,* which he insisted could only be understood in a revolutionary context: the flames that engulf Valhalla are the revolutionary flames that were soon to consume the existing order. While broke and in exile in 1849, Wagner wrote, "My task is this: to bring revolution wherever I go." Historian Jacques Barzun describes Wagner as "drunk" at this time with "vindictiveness against the Philistinism of the opera-going bourgeoisie,"[4] which is an excellent, indeed exact, description of resentment of the economic kind, which explains Wagner's socialist rhetoric.

However, Wagner's revolutionary ardor began to gradually falter under the burden of ever-increasing poverty and debts, and appears to have vanished without a trace after young King Ludwig of Bavaria became Wagner's royal patron immediately upon acceding to his throne. Even before his first wife died, Wagner became involved in a scandalous affair with Cosima Von Bulow, the daughter of Franz Liszt and the wife of Wagner's own chief assistant and musical disciple, the young conductor Hans Von Bulow. After the death of Wagner's first wife, Cosima converted from Catholicism to Protestantism in order to obtain a divorce from Hans, then promptly married Wagner.

During the long interruption in Wagner's work on *The Ring,* when he wrote *Tristan und Isolde* and *Die Meistersinger,* Wagner's views unquestionably underwent major changes. Gone was the early revolutionary, antimonarchist tone. *Die Meistersinger* closes on an ultra-nationalist note with a paen to "holy German art." (This passage appears to have been put in at Cosima's strong urging, against Wagner's better judgment.)[5] Wagner's conversations and writings began to take on a profoundly anti-Semitic tone, no doubt influenced by Cosima's strong anti-Semitism. He became ecstatic over the Prussian victory over France in 1870 and by the unification of Germany under the Prussian monarchy the following year. In 1871, Wagner even wrote a "Kaiser March" to celebrate the unification of Germany under the Prussian king. Gone was the atheistic, socialist revolutionary, but Wagner was clearly still a revolutionary of a very different kind.

In *The Perfect Wagnerite,* George Bernard Shaw, a pious socialist, heaps scorn on the post-*Tristan* Wagner for having sold out his earlier revolutionary ideals.[6] Shaw depicts the earlier parts of *The Ring* as a searing indictment of the nineteenth-century capitalist system, an interpretation which is undoubtedly correct. Shaw interprets the *Tarnhelm*—a helmet of magical transformation that enables the dwarf Alberich to dominate the subterranean dwarf-land of Nibelheim—as a representation of the capitalist's tall silk hat, the sign of their domination over the workers. Nibelheim itself, where the dwarfs must toil endlessly in darkness for their master, is of course the factory. The Gods' magnificent residence up in the clouds in Valhalla symbolizes the villas of wealthy industrialists.

The point is clear—sometime between 1848 and 1871, Richard Wagner, undoubtedly swayed by the strong-willed Cosima, traded one set of resentments for another and converted from socialism to what we would today call fascism, a form of ultranationalism with strong religious overtones. Generic fascism is based on powerful resentments against prosperous foreigners, and especially "foreign believers" (in this case, the Jews) who are successful enough to embarrass native nonachievers, who like to think of themselves as special not because they have accomplished anything but because they belong to a "superior" race or nation and hold the "correct" religion. (Hitler was a "self-admitted former derelict" who found a rather direct way to the top.[7] If the most flamboyant derelict currently living in a flophouse in the slums of your town were to somehow seize and hold unlimited power, the outcome would be much the same.) We thus see how twentieth-century fascism was the distillate of nineteenth-century "heroic" revolutionary romanticism, which came to assume a profoundly nationalistic character, leading inexorably to two world wars.

The link between the powerful Wagnerian movement and national socialism is obvious and indisputable. Wagner's *Lohengrin* was Hitler's favorite opera, and he listened to it many times during his youth.[8] He fancied himself a knight like Lohengrin, defending German honor. "Arise! With God for the honor of our German Reich," the German knights sing. It is not difficult to envision the infatuation this opera would induce in the future fuehrer. Hitler was a frequent guest at the Wagner family home in Bayreuth in the years before he came to power, and he infatuated Wagner's daughter-in-law Winifred Wagner. She was later in charge of the "sacred festival music" at Bayreuth (no mere opera house, this). Winifred Wagner kept her enthusiasm for Hitler and his cause until the time of her death in 1980. Her son Wieland said of her in 1975, "she still believes in the final victory of the fuehrer."[9]

That other late-to-be-unified country, Italy, which possessed the only other great and supremely unifying national opera of the nineteenth century, also became fascist a half-century or so after it first became a nation. It is clear that the intensely nationalistic operas of Giuseppi Verdi must have provided an impulse in this dangerous direction—the mystical worship of the state and race—although nowhere as powerful as that of Wagner in Germany. Whether the intensely nationalistic opera in Germany and Italy was a principal cause of the rise of fascism or merely a reflection of its rising fervor is difficult to say for certain, although it would be hard to deny that music played at least a contributing role. What the careers of Wagner and Verdi clearly demonstrate is that seemingly innocuous music can carry with it a powerful philosophy, profoundly motivating people for good or for ill, and thus can have far-reaching consequences. In our own time, rock music energizes and unites the resentful, driving them onward to excesses, just as Wagner's music of German ultranationalism united and drove onward those infatuated with the German *Volk und Reich.*

Artists once spent their time in pursuit of the sublime, the beautiful (for was that not once the definition of an artist?), and almost as a by-product they created works that became highly prized by the *nouveau riche,* whose artistic knowledge and discernment did not always match their disposable incomes. Artists, perceiving this, understandably became uneasy. "They, the rich, have so much money to spend on art; even on bad art: We, however, have far better artistic knowledge and judgment, yet we are virtually penniless." It seems so unfair, at least to those who never stop to consider that the *nouveau riche* gained their money through the fanatical pursuit of excellence in the kind of work that requires high pay to keep someone doing it. Artists, on the other hand, have opted to spend their lives in far more interesting and pleasant pursuits, in spite of the near-certain prospect of penury. The wealthy collector buying their paintings may have had to endure extreme stress and fatigue for the last forty years to earn his money. But such thoughts never occur to persons who are ignorant of economics, and thus as economic growth accelerated, resentment among artists grew. Almost imperceptibly resentment began to worm its way into the fabric of art itself.

Now art exists almost solely to shock, and for the artist it is obligatory to hold views that are "politically correct" in their entirety. (This interesting concept of being "politically correct" was, of course, invented and perpetuated by the resentful themselves. It is a latter-day *nihil obstat,* certifying the possessor's views to be free from doctrinal or moral errors; that is, certifying that this person sides with resentment against achievement on every issue.) This makes for an interesting game, perhaps even an amusing farce, but it is not art. Thus we now understand another major reason that the creation of great art has now all but ceased. All art has become politicized, overtly so in totalitarian regimes, more subtly elsewhere; so that, at present, art that is void of resentment is unacceptable to the contemporary artistic community. Any work of music, poetry, painting, or whatever, that is not sufficiently shocking to the economically responsible class is perceived by the art-bohemians as inanely saccharine, as void of "social relevance," an inexcusable sell-out to monied interests. (*Il faut épater la bourgeoisie,* or else it isn't art, my friend.) And when art allowed its meaning to be warped from the pursuit of sublime beauty to the blind rage against material success, art as it once existed simply ceased to be.

THE ARTS

To judge by the almost uniformly dismal state of modern art, the degree of thought-control within that craft must rival that in the Gulag. Not the slightest deviation from the party line—i.e., not the least expression of pride in achievement or beauty for its own sake—is permitted. Of course many of the greatest artists of the past cared nothing for the arbitrary dictates that prevailed at the time: One laughs to think of a Beethoven, a Wagner, or a Voltaire striving to be perceived as "politically correct" by his peers. The present age probably does not lack artists of ability, but it certainly lacks artists of courage. Until some artist of indisputable talent and almost superhuman courage bursts forth from the bonds of convention and creates a work that expresses the pride of civilization's great achievers, unapologetic in its pursuit of beauty and noble grace, giving its own unique expression to some unchanging facet of human existence, art will remain mired in resentment, a game played by aged adolescents still seeking to smite their parents with the greatest blow for which no retaliation will be forthcoming.

NOTES

1. Emerson, Ralph Waldo, "The Poet" (in *Essays,* second series, 1844).
2. Wolfe, Tom, *The Painted Word* (New York: Farrar, Straus & Giroux, 1975), chapter 3.
3. Magee, Brian, *Aspects of Wagner* (New York: Stein & Day, 1969).
4. Barzun, Jacques. *Darwin, Marx, Wagner* (Boston: Little, Brown, 1941), part 3, chapter 1.
5. James, Burnett, *Wagner and the Romantic Disaster* (New York: Hippocrene Books, 1983), chapter 7.

6. Shaw, George Bernard, *The Perfect Wagnerite* (New York: Dover, 1967).

7. Arendt, Hannah, *Totalitarianism* (New York: Harcourt, Brace, & World, 1968), chapter 1.

8. Toland, John, *Adolph Hitler* (New York: Doubleday, 1976), chapters 1, 2.

9. *Washington Post,* March 7, 1980, obituary for Winifred Wagner. For all her nationalistic fervor, Winifred wasn't even a native-born German (neither, of course, was Hitler). She was born in Britain, but was adopted as a small child by a German musician. She married Siegfried Wagner, son of the composer, in 1915; she was 17, he was 46.

7.
Politics and Conflict

In talking about political groups and movements, many people think in terms of liberals vs. conservatives, or of liberty vs. totalitarianism, or of democracy vs. Marxism. Such concepts have not only been seriously overused and hence are losing their ability to arouse or change thinking, but there are also many significant movements that do not seem to fit in. For example, can it really be that fascism and Marxism-Leninism are opposites when they have so much in common that they are, in many ways, hardly distinguishable? Similarly, how do we reconcile a phenomenon like Islamic fundamentalism, which is presumably ultra-conservative yet can have strong ties to Marxism, which is presumably ultra-liberal? (For example, the present government of Syria.)

POLITICS AND CONFLICT

Many people picture the political spectrum as a uni-dimensional line something like this:

Marxists	Socialists	Democrats	Republicans	KKK	Nazis
LEFT		CENTER			RIGHT

Clearly, this model is worthless. The very concept of left vs. right is two hundred years old, originating at the French National Assembly when the nobility demanded the privilege of being seated on the speaker's right. Those on the right today do not, of course, demand any special privileges for nobility of birth. They are typically not consistent in demanding anything at all. They say they want to see the generation of wealth through free-market principles, but at the same time they promote a religion which would condemn to everlasting torment anyone who actually did so.

Why is anti-Semitism rampant at both ends of the spectrum? Where do we place libertarians? Why do groups outside the presumed center (democracy) hate democracy so much? Why is there always a migration out of socialist countries into free-market countries whenever it is possible to do so? (If socialism really did benefit the poor, the opposite would happen: Poor people from the capitalist U.S.—who are always free to leave— would be emigrating to more socialist countries, like Mexico, and especially to Cuba. What a laugh! When will our so-called "intellectuals" find the courage to openly admit that capitalism benefits the poor?) Why are many countries that were never colonized by the U.S., were never opposed by the U.S., and in fact are often the recipient of generous aid from the U.S., nonetheless rabidly anti-American? Such questions have no satisfactory answers in conventional political thinking.

Other people use an obviously more sophisticated two-dimensional model, which addresses some of the objections raised above:

POLITICAL FREEDOM	ECONOMIC FREEDOM: FOR	ECONOMIC FREEDOM: AGAINST
FOR	Libertarians	Socialists w/Human Face Liberals The "Counterculture"
AGAINST	Conservatives Fascists	Marxists

But even this improved model will not work. There are still elements that simply do not fit in. (For example, many Christian fundamentalists, who clearly cannot be lumped with Marxists or even with conservatives because of their populist, anti-intellectual, anti-business orientation, oppose both personal and economic freedom.) To no one's surprise, I propose that a more intelligible model—one that sheds more light on contemporary issues—must be understood in terms of "resentment against achievement":

POLITICS AND CONFLICT

MORALITY

	HUMAN-DERIVED	"DIVINELY GIVEN"
ACHIEVEMENT-ORIENTED	Libertarians Nietzsche Ayn Rand Voltaire	Conservatives William F. Buckley Main-Line Protestants Republicans
RESENTMENT-ORIENTED	Marxists Socialists Fascists	Democrats Christian Fundamentalists Islamic Fundamentalists

What is *taxation?* Some people say "taxation is theft." Others say taxes are the dues we must pay under "the social contract." However, I suggest that, to a first approximation, taxation can be regarded as the financial cost of resentment to achievement. It is true that at least some of our tax money goes to pay for genuinely useful things: medical research, building roads, operating schools, and so on. It has been suggested by some that taxation is not the best way for such services to be funded. Setting aside that question for now, it is clear that apart from a certain number of useful services, most of our tax dollars go either to subsidizing resentment, or else to defending against it.

The dollars that go into income redistribution programs subsidize nonviolent domestic resentment, enabling the resentful to largely avoid the discipline of work. This is in essence a bribe intended to keep them placated. Foreign aid is a similar bribe to nonviolent foreign resentment, trying to buy friends with a display of magnanimity and strength. (Of course, by flaunting

140

our powerfulness, resentment against us can only increase.) Law enforcement programs and prisons are the price we pay to keep violent domestic resentment in check and to limit the damage it does to law-abiding citizens. And our defense establishment exists almost solely to defend our achievement-oriented society against the "international class struggle" ceaselessly being waged by a profoundly resentful proletarian state, in the absence of which we could drastically reduce our defense expenditures.

And it is achievement that must pay the full cost of this. Only achievement can be taxed, since resentment produces nothing of value. You cannot tax resentment, for envy and hatred never result in anything positive; resentment can survive only as a parasite upon acquiescent achievement. Thus the members of the economically responsible class must pay not only the full and unsubsidized cost of their own personal expenses (which include family expenses as well as any voluntary contributions to charities), but they are additionally compelled to pay both the subsidies to nonviolent resentment (welfare and foreign aid) and the cost of the common defense against the violently resentful (law enforcement and national defense).

Various "income redistribution" programs seek to disguise the fact that no one can enjoy a standard of living higher than that dictated by his or her own productivity unless someone else is penalized to subsidize the difference. Economics says to everyone, regardless of race, creed, sex, or any other factor, "If you want a higher standard of living, you must become more productive. To generate affluence, give value for value." Psychologically, the resentful must escape the painful and acutely embarrassing fact that their standard of living, dismally low as it is, is in fact far more than they actually earn; for not only do the profoundly resentful typically have very low productivity— or none at all—but in many cases their productivity is actually negative, meaning that they would steal from an employer, and vandalize his property. It actually imposes a net cost on a company to have such people around, well beyond whatever they may be paid.

Socialism is that scheme that seeks to harness and exploit the superior achiever for the benefit of the inferior. Of course, the superior achiever seeks to escape this servitude if he can. Hence a "brain drain" is suffered by partly socialist countries, while the Berlin Wall becomes a necessity where resentment's triumph has been complete. When superior achievers cannot escape such predations, they simply sink down in lassitude, practice perfect Christian-style submission, and become indistinguishable from the rest of the herd. When a society becomes mired in socialism, no class—neither rich nor poor—actually benefits. Achievers derive little advantage from their exertions and hence gradually stop trying, while the resentful find that there remains practically no achievement left in that society to exploit.

In domestic politics, the struggle of resentment against achievement roughly parallels the liberal/conservative struggle, which is the principal battle line of the political parties. The result is two firmly entrenched major parties and no significant minor ones. Many Democrats, as members of a party leaning strongly toward resentment against wealth, seek to increase subsidies to domestic resentment by placing increasingly large levies on successful achievement, and they are reluctant to oppose the predations and extortions of international resentment. However, they do not wish to entirely confiscate the rewards of individual initiative. They seek to survive as wise parasites, who are careful not to kill their host. Republicans, on the other hand, who identify much more strongly with achievement, seek to decrease the size of the levy upon achievement and are far more willing to defend against the continuing assaults of international resentment, but they are still willing to subsidize domestic resentment to a considerable degree. Unfortunately, most Republicans subscribe to a pious Christian morality, and hence see the poor as virtuous.

Democracy as it is practiced today in North America and in Western Europe represents an uneasy compromise between resentment and achievement. Achievement is protected from total confiscation in return for its willingness to turn over a quarter, a third, or even more of its earnings to resentment. While we are fortunate that our political liberties remain largely intact, the once ironclad protection of property rights, which the Founding Fathers wrote into the Constitution, have been eroded by two centuries of covetous assault by the politics of resentment, turning what was once a magnificent edifice for the protection of achievement into a scheme for milking it. When achievement-oriented values prevail, people may keep what they hold and what they earn, except for a small self-assessed fee for the common defense against resentment, foreign and domestic. However, when we see achievers being milked like cows, it is a clear sign that proletarian theft-oriented values have infected the body politic.

Domestically, law enforcement is hampered by the fact that those steeped in resentment-morality are reluctant to have our laws be too rigidly enforced or to enforce penalties commensurate with the severity of the offense. This is because nearly all serious criminal offenses are committed by the poor, and resentment-morality teaches that the poor are the "good" people. Thus many perfectly sincere and honest individuals are deeply troubled because, while they understand that law enforcement is needed to ensure the survival of civilization, the law is forever punishing those they believe to be "good" (the undisciplined indigent) and protecting those they believe to be "wicked" (those who have assets worth stealing). They come to genuinely believe that our society must itself be wicked because it is forever punishing "the blessed" and "the exploited" while protecting "the exploiter," whose entry into heaven must be preceded by a camel passing through a needle's eye. This distressing conclusion does indeed follow from the premises they have accepted.

The apparent paradox is resolved, however, when we recognize that resentment-morality is the inversion of the morality of achievement, that envy does not justify theft, and that civilization must protect achievement in order to survive. Those chronically on the wrong side of the law are those who are too undisciplined to refrain from predatory acts. They believe that wealth is best acquired by clever theft as the opportunity arises, not by the diligent, truthful pursuit of long-term business and employment relationships. To the achiever, virtue consists not of a life of hustles and scams, punctuated by robberies and violent acts, but of praiseworthy achievement, carried out in a context of lawful behavior. Thus law enforcement is indeed on the side of morality and is doing exactly what needs to be done, which is to incarcerate those whose resentments are too violent to control. The achiever does not swoon with pity and brotherly love for violent criminals, but instead is filled with loathing and disgust that any human being should act so savagely. The achiever sympathizes instead with the innocent person who has been unjustly robbed, assaulted, injured, or even killed by the violent criminal.

Savages who have committed violent crimes have already done greater harm than would be done by keeping them in prison the rest of their lives, or even by executing them. The savage has harmed or killed a good person, an innocent, who did no harm to anyone. Surely any rational system of morality must value the life, health, and interests of those who obey its dictates more highly than that of those who flaunt them: To do otherwise would make it an anti-morality, penalizing those who follow it. But resentment-morality is more worried about the future happiness and liberty of the savage than about the harm that has befallen the innocent victim; so it tries to get violent offenders (undisciplined, hence good) out of prison quickly, with as little inconvenience to them as possible. This gives them the opportunity to strike again—for indeed most serious crimes are committed by those who have previously been convicted of one or more serious criminal acts. Resentment's pity for the savage far outweighs any consideration of what this vicious animal will likely do if it is turned loose again. (But even one future assault against a good person counts for far more than what happens to the bad. If we must err, let it be on the side of the good.)

Unfortunately, domestic resentment resonates in profound sympathy with foreign resentment, since both perceive a common enemy: the capitalist achiever. Both share a common sense of outrage that anyone should be permitted to earn and accumulate wealth through honest work. Therefore, domestic resentment reflexively resists the efforts required to defend achievement against its implacable foreign enemies. They hear the incessant Marxist-Leninist attacks upon capitalist achievers and discern within them strong parallels to their own resentments against wealth. Many of them come to subconsciously perceive themselves as having greater sympathies with the enemies of democratic capitalism than with its defenders. Then when international resentment launches some new assault to expand its anticapitalist empire (in Cuba, Vietnam, Nicaragua, Angola, or wherever), domestic resentment vigorously opposes all efforts to resist this expansion. Since the majority political party in the United States leans profoundly toward resentment, the futility of all such resistance is thereby guaranteed.

Domestic resentment insists that all apparent treaty violations by the Soviets cannot possibly be true, and that the only reason we do not have harmonious relations with the Soviets is that we have not made enough concessions. They reason that if the Soviets are resentful (in political terms, "progressive") like ourselves, must they not share our good intentions? (And many of these naive leftists genuinely do have good intentions; they have not thought through their proposals to see the mass arrests and the regimentation that socialism inevitably entails.) They naively imagine that even if the worst should happen, at least some good might come of it, and they personally would be spared any unpleasant consequences, due to their lifelong left-of-center orientation. They are blissfully ignorant of the fact that rival nonorthodox leftists were among the very first groups Lenin ordered sent to his new death-through-work camps; such people can never be counted on to do as they are ordered.

ROBERT SHEAFFER

One popular channel for expressing resentment against successful foreigners is in the area of international trade. This usually takes the form of a jingoistic attempt to "save" the domestic economy from "unfair" (i.e., more efficient) foreign competition. Foreigner-bashing often has strong appeal among marginal achievers, who can thus blame their own lack of economic success upon foreign devils. The owners and managers of unsuccessful businesses have also been known to get on this bandwagon. Political candidates can safely engage in small-scale demagoguery by fanning the flames of resentment against high-achieving foreigners, who are not eligible to vote in domestic elections. Sometimes appeals to stop foreign commerce are coupled with strong appeals to "national awareness," and these are often tinged with anti-Semitism—two key elements of fascism, that flavor of resentment appealing to those who have more "racial purity" than they have brains.

Whenever you see people who harbor powerful racial prejudices, you can be certain that their achievements are marginal to nonexistent. They have to keep reminding themselves that they are indeed "better" than some other group, because there is good reason to suspect otherwise; they appear to be at or near the very bottom of the economic ladder. Hence, the constant stroking of their pathetic ego, the continual self-reassurance that they are somehow "better" than that other hated group (it doesn't matter which) merely because of the color of their skin or some other accident of birth. Of course, there is nothing wrong with feeling good about one's group and its accomplishments, but when these feelings fuse into a metaphysical assertion of "special insight" or "innate superiority," it is extremely dangerous. People who are inordinately proud of their "race" or "blood" are clearly proclaiming that their lives contain no *real* accomplishments to be proud of. Hence, they must fall back upon mystical doctrines to attempt to refute the obvious fact that they are indeed the losers they appear to be.

Why do we have wars? One popular explanation holds that war is a consequence of capitalist greed. The Marxists say that as capitalism grinds away toward its inexorable decline, increasingly desperate capitalist nations go to war with each other to expand their colonial empires for the eagerly sought prize of being able to sell their "overproduction" to the colonials. (One might object that this makes absolutely no sense, since the natives of the colonies have practically no money with which to buy anything. But Lenin has an answer to this: he says that we capitalists forcibly "export" our capital into our colonies, which apparently forces them to buy our overproduced goods from us with our own money.[1] The so-called colonials, however, are now getting the last laugh: there seems to be no way to make them pay back the loan.) This view never had much evidence to support it and would seem today to have an insurmountable problem in that the only remaining old-fashioned colonial empire belongs to the Soviet Union. The hypothesis linking capitalism and war was definitively refuted when Communist China fought Communist Vietnam, when Communist China and the Communist USSR began to see each other as enemies (they may someday fight), and when Communist Vietnam invaded and conquered Communist Cambodia. The fact that some people still believe that "capitalism causes war" tells us nothing except the quality of thought among certain so-called intellectuals.

ROBERT SHEAFFER

Wars are caused by unscrupulous and megalomanic rulers, who hold the kind of theft-oriented values that typify the proletariat. Such rulers are not answerable to any electorate, to any legislature, or to anything else except their own urges and/ or delusions. Such people, when holding power, do not even know the meaning of words like fairness or magnanimity. Wars are started by rulers such as these, by Hitlers and Napoleons, by Caesars and Stalins and Qaddafis—but never by Chamberlins, Roosevelts, Churchills, Carters, or Brandts. No elected leader has ever started a war against a peaceful neighbor; in fact, democracies are slow to defend themselves even when provoked, and they waste much valuable time and effort pretending that megalomania or virulent ideology can be "negotiated" out of existence. But unelected, nonconsensual leaders (i.e., those unscrupulous enough to obtain their positions through a combination of deception and force), come to believe that to be a formula for success, and they seek to expand their power in a like manner. Many intellectuals are credulous enough to believe that regimes that seize power through the most vicious coups and maintain it through the most violent internal repression are nonetheless nonthreatening—nay, positively angelic—when it comes to foreign policy. This delusion, which is akin to a belief in Santa Claus, is once again nothing more than the time-honored error of judging unscrupulous scoundrels by the high standards that prevail in one's own professional circles.

The solution to war is rule by consent of the governed, when free people are allowed to rule themselves. In a republic, leaders can act only through consensus, and since the people (not the leaders) always suffer the most in any war, a consensus for war (unless directly attacked) is virtually impossible to obtain. In a world in which all peoples were self-ruled, war would disappear—just as it already has among the democratic nations of the world; for to have a functioning democracy, the electorate must be, on the whole, truthful enough to abide by negotiation and compromise, and thus all disputes really can be settled using nonviolent options. England, France, West Germany, Italy, the United States, Japan—all are formerly warring nations, but they will never go to war with each other again, at least not as long as their present form of government is preserved.

The greatest hijacking of all time occurred when a radical terrorist group along the lines of the PLO or the Red Brigades succeeded in hijacking not merely a ship or an airplane but the crumbling empire of a confused and deluded Russian czar. Since then, many people have mistaken that terrorist band for a government, an error which suits its purposes fine, but the relationship is, and always has been, not that of a legitimate government and loyal citizens but that of terrorists and hostages. None may leave the USSR without permission—a situation virtually without historical precedent among legitimate governments, but routine in hijackings. Arbitrary executions of persons arbitrarily arrested are not to be questioned. The entire gross national product of the country—such as it is—belongs to the hijackers, to be used however they see fit. The highest priority is the "ideological struggle," which implies nothing less than the remaking of the rest of the world into the image of the USSR. The majority of the people must tolerate living standards far behind those of the capitalist world, with absolutely no recourse, in order to finance this mad expansion. Just as a virus invades a living cell in order to turn that cell into a factory whose sole purpose is the replication of that virus, which destroys the cell in the process, the Bolshevik virus has turned the empire of the late czar into a machine whose single-minded goal is not the improvement of the lives and fortunes of its people but the spread of the virus.

Consider Solzhenitsyn's description of how "Soviet power" was consolidated. In *The Gulag Archipelago,* he notes the arrests of "tens of thousands of *hostages,* i.e., people not personally accused of anything, those peaceful citizens not even listed by name, who were taken off and destroyed simply to terrorize or wreak vengeance on a military enemy or a rebellious population. After August 30, 1918, the NKVD (later to become the KGB) ordered the localities to 'arrest immediately *all* Right Socialist Revolutionaries and to take *a significant number of hostages* from the bourgeoisie and military officers.' [emphasis in original]." Solzhenitsyn further notes that "by a decree of the Defense Council of February 15, 1919—apparently with Lenin in the chair—the Cheka and the NKVD were ordered to take hostage *peasants* from those localities where the removal of snow from railroad tracks 'was not proceeding satisfactorily,' and 'if the snow removal did not take place they were to be shot.' "[2]

Elsewhere in *The Gulag Archipelago,* Solzhenitsyn tells the history of certain individuals taken hostage by Lenin's terrorists after seizing power. Pyotar Palchinsky, a prominent mining engineer, was "arrested without charges" in June of 1918. On September 6, his name was included on a list of 122 prominent hostages publicly posted. The note read, "If even one Soviet official is killed, the hostages listed below will be shot. Signed: Petrograd

Cheka; G. Boky, Chairman." (In civilized countries, of course, it is unthinkable for the law to punish (let alone kill) a person merely to influence the action of another. Such are our bourgeois prejudices.) Nor did such atrocities end when the Soviet regime had achieved firm control. Solzhenitsyn tells how in 1925, during the supposedly humane "New Economic Policy" (the Soviets' first flirtation with *glasnost*), a nonorthodox socialist fled to avoid arrest, and his wife and her best friend were taken hostage to force his return.[3]

Is this how a government comes to power, or is this a hijacking by a terrorist band? Anyone who mistakes Lenin's terrorists for a legitimate government should read *The Gulag Archipelago* to be disabused of that notion. Millions were exterminated, not for any crime or act of opposition but for the "crime" of belonging to a social class that didn't appreciate socialism. (Orthodox Marxists correctly perceive that it is impossible to convince the hard-working, upwardly mobile bourgeoisie that the resentments of the indigent have merit; they know the source of their own success and that anyone else could have done the same, with the same degree of determination and planning. Hence, the physical extermination of the bourgeoisie is the only way to eradicate this mentality.) There is no more legitimacy to such a "government" than there is to the iron rule over airplane passengers by terrorists. The duration and scope of a hijacking do not confer legitimacy upon it, but instead hint at its ruthlessness. Furthermore, any area patrolled by guards to prevent escape is a prison, regardless of its size. Soviet "citizens" are docile for the same reason as are passengers on a hijacked airplane—it is the only way to survive.

When other terrorist groups employ these same ruthless

tactics today, they are simply trying to emulate Lenin's success. Hostage-taking is a very successful means of exploiting noble behavior, which respects the lives of individuals, by proletarian savagery, which does not. Terrorists are typically fighting for the One True Faith and/or Racial Blood (sometimes National Blood), and they will commit any act of savagery to drive out Foreign Blood, Infidel Blood. The idea that any thinking person can consider this "progressive" or romantic is absurd (although it is obvious that this is fully consistent with the irrational nationalist and racialist mania of romanticism—that revolt of the jingoistic, nationalistic nineteenth and twentieth centuries against the rationalist cosmopolitanism of the eighteenth century.) The PLO is fighting for the same goals as the KKK: religious intolerance and racial bigotry. *Civilized* people tolerate ethnic, racial, and religious diversities. Any "liberation" group fighting against persons more tolerant and more productive than themselves is fighting on the wrong side.

Such brutal tactics are in widespread use today by Islamic fundamentalists, who harbor vicious resentments against those in their society who have gained wealth and power through the adoption of Western ("worldly") values. The tactic has been nearly as successful for them as it was for Lenin: Both the Reagan administration and the Israeli government, while pretending to be "tough" on terrorists, have in fact sent arms to Iran in exchange for hostages. It should surprise no one that Islamic resentment strikes out most savagely against that group which, coming into that same barren Middle Eastern desert where Allah's people have lived in wretched poverty for centuries, has in a few decades turned it into a modern, prosperous, industrialized country.

POLITICS AND CONFLICT

In the "class struggle" (i.e., the continuing assault of resentment against achievement) a person's moral worth is determined by his birth, not by his actions, thus re-establishing a hierarchy based on birth, albeit now inverted. Thieves are considered "socially friendly" (i.e., resentment-oriented) elements, for the Marxists agree with me that the thief exemplifies sturdy proletarian values. Thieves were treated relatively leniently in the Gulag camps, often supervising the "socially hostile" (achievement-oriented) prisoners, such as engineers or businessmen. The radical writer Maxim Gorky, speaking to a work brigade of such thieves, shouted "after all, any capitalist steals more than all of you combined!"[4]

Educated people were invariably on the losing end of the Soviet "class struggle." "Engineers were looked on as a socially suspicious element that did not even have the right to provide an education for its own children," writes Solzhenitsyn. In the factory, while engineers were held accountable for meeting schedules and quotas, "any worker could not only refuse to carry out the instructions of an engineer, but could insult and strike him and go unpunished—and as a representative of the ruling class the worker was *always right* in such a case." Despite its protestations, resentment does not actually seek to abolish hierarchies, but to invert them. As for those intellectuals who imagine that the socialism they admire from afar might perhaps increase their meager prestige, they should consider Lenin's reply to Gorky, who had attempted to intercede in ongoing mass-arrests of the intelligentsia: "In actual fact, they are not (the nation's) brains, but shit."[5] The enemy in the "class war" is anyone who has demonstrated any noticeable achievement in any field whatsoever, even if he never earned much money in doing so.

Indeed, Soviet penal philosophy has officially stated that the notion of "individual guilt" is an antiquated bourgeois concept. Properly "class conscious" thinking asks not what actual harm a person has done but what harm a person from such a social element might do if left unshot! As Solzhenitsyn explains, "The heart of the matter is not personal guilt but social danger." The infamous Soviet prosecutor Andrei Y. Vyshinsky warned against the "bourgeois weighing of punishments in relation to the gravity of what has been committed." The concept might be thought of as a kind of "preventive extermination"—resentment carried to its logical extreme. (These are the people now pointing hydrogen bombs at your city. Some people claim we are too suspicious of their intentions.) By the way, if you, the reader, happen to have a college degree, you too can be sentenced as a member of a socially dangerous element—the "individual nobility"—for having risen so far beyond the proletariat, no matter how modest the circumstances of your birth.[6] Your "class consciousness" has by now been hopelessly polluted by elitist thought. This same mad logic was later applied in China by Mao Tse-Tung, resulting in the destruction of the university system and the Chinese economy for an entire generation, and later still in Cambodia by Pol Pot.

Because resentment is impotent and incapable of creating anything worthwhile, it can survive only as a parasite upon achievement. The cooperation of internal achievement can be obtained, albeit reluctantly, by the fact that not only have "the means of production" been nationalized, but the populace as well. Given that no one is allowed to leave, the best one can hope for are the pitifully small material rewards given Soviet achievers—perhaps a separate apartment for one's married children, or a new refrigerator. However, deceptive ploys need to be used by societies based on the resentments of life's failures to obtain wealth and assistance from success-oriented societies; that is, societies where achievement for private gain is legal. Thus far, the two most useful ploys have been the taking of hostages, which exploits the civilized person's respect for human life, and the suggestion or threat of military conflict, which exploits every self-ruled people's unfailing desire to be left in peace.

Indeed, the taking and holding of hostages is essential to the establishment and operation of a proletarian state; such a state cannot continue to function without them. In fact, it would not be too great an oversimplification to characterize Marxism-Leninism as "that faction of Marxism which utilizes the taking of hostages to seize and hold power." Not only did the Soviet government make widespread use of the taking of hostages in its initial consolidation of power, but even today, when it is necessary for a "citizen" (i.e., one of the nationalized "means of production") of the USSR or a country in its colonial empire to go abroad, in nearly every case at least one family member must remain behind as a hostage.

The West German government has for years been paying significant sums of money to East Germany to allow a small number of "citizens" to emigrate (paying ransom for hostages, bluntly speaking). According to Jean-François Revel, at least some of this ransom money has been traced to "peace" groups in the West, which use it to attempt to weaken the West's capability or resolve to defend itself. Other communist countries have done the same. Romanian communist party boss Nicolae Ceaucsescu boasted to his aides that "Oil, Jews, and Germans are our most important export commodities." Any U.S. citizen applying for a security clearance will find it nearly impossible to obtain if he has relatives living in Marxist countries, because the American would likely be threatened with harm to his relatives (the hostages) should he refuse to supply classified information to the USSR. When the U.S., or some other Western country, arrests a Soviet spy who is not protected by diplomatic immunity, the Soviets arrest as a "spy" some innocent person of that nationality who happens to be in the Soviet Union at that time (remember Nicholas Daniloff?), and then they agree to an exchange of "spies."[7] The innocent person serves as a convenient hostage for the Soviet state, but only for use as a weapon against civilized countries. When dealing with a regime as savage as their own, such as that of Hitler or Khomeini, the ploy is rendered useless, for neither side respects human lives. And, of course, Soviet-sponsored terrorists who attack Western interests are of great value in weakening and demoralizing states where achievement for private gain is legal.

The other great international ploy for extracting wealth from achievement is to plant the idea that loans, favorable trade arrangements, and other forms of financial assistance are necessary to preserve "better relations" and avoid the danger of global war. This is a thinly disguised form of tribute extorted from us.

A moment's reflection should serve to refute the line of reasoning that says that both the U.S. and the USSR "want peace" but "don't trust each other," and hence must sit down and "reach agreements" that will increase trust and understanding.

The concept of negotiating in good faith is a bourgeois concept, a derivative of the aristocratic code of a gentleman honoring his word. This concept is utterly alien to a proletarian state. The proletarian counterpart is to employ cunning and deceit to gain short-term advantage, a concept put into practice every day in the slums of our major cities in the form of scams too numerous to count, and by the Soviets by violating every major treaty they have ever signed if there was the slightest advantage in doing so. They know we never hold them accountable for such actions. The Soviets have obviously concluded that a treaty is a useful trick for gaining advantage over the West. "If we don't sign treaties and play hard to get when they want better relations, they will try to coax us into treaties and we can extract more concessions from them. On the other hand, when we do sign treaties, we can get away with cheating and they can't. Either way, we come out ahead."

Do not forget that the Soviets have solemnly pledged not to interfere in the governments of eastern Europe; to allow the free movement of people between East and West Berlin; to allow its "citizens" to freely monitor human rights abuses; to not use chemical or biological weapons; to refrain from interference with international radio broadcasts, and so on. Not a day goes by without the Soviets violating at least one of these "solemn" treaties. To sign more treaties with them at this time would be a sign of utter imbecility; we should insist that they stop cheating on the treaties they have already signed as a precondition for signing any more.

Because of our own nobility of thought, we habitually try to think the best about everyone else, even our adversaries. We mistakenly conclude that because we have no malice, we must have no enemies. This represents a fundamental misunderstanding of resentment, which is the hatred and envy of success. Resentment survives by the exploitation of noble behavior, by the continued error of the higher classes in judging proletarian actions by the same high standards of fairness and trust prevailing in their own circles. In dealing with an adversary who has consistenty demonstrated such ignoble traits as mendacity and brutality in the extreme, one must always assume the worst, until such time as the fury of the enemy's resentment is eventually dissolved by the necessity of sustaining—and rewarding—its own achievers. Thus "arms control" treaties cannot be trusted in circumstances when they are needed, and are not needed in circumstances when they can be trusted.

Why is there no nuclear arms race between the U.S. and Britain—nations that are now on good terms but have fought in the past? Why do we not even dream of a possible first strike coming from the U.K.? For that matter, why do not the British fear the French in the slightest, or vice versa? Why do neither of them fear us? Each nation possesses enough nuclear weapons to destroy the major cities of the other, and they have been adversaries on and off for centuries. Can it be because each instinctively realizes that the other is a bourgeois democracy, and thus is fundamentally truthful, embodying civilized values such as tolerance, rule by consensus, justice, and non-aggression, reflecting the makeup of its electorate?

Democracies are as docile as cows. We know that, and our enemies know that, too. If they perceived us as the least bit dangerous, they would be hesitant to make up lies about us.

"Let's not provoke those Americans with fabricated charges— they might do something rash." Such would be Soviet policy *if* they perceived us as threatening in the least. The fact that the Soviet propaganda organs are constantly reporting fictional atrocities by the U.S. (such as allegedly locking up illegal Mexican immigrants in forced-labor camps, using poison gas against civilians in Grenada, brutally suppressing peaceful protest, and so on) demonstrates conclusively that they don't perceive us as any kind of threat whatsoever, but rather as an adversary who can safely be punched and prodded, provided that they are careful not to punch too hard. This is the universal action of resentment: to strike the greatest blow that will not be retaliated. By not reacting to such lies in any way, we create a large zone of free attack, giving those who resent us license to defame us as much as they please.

On the other hand, when we truthfully point to objectionable behavior on the part of the Soviets, apologists of international resentment accuse us of spoiling the chance for "better relations." But if the Soviets actually desired "better relations," they could easily signal it by refraining from telling crude lies about us to the rest of the world. For example, in 1986, during Gorbachev's policy of alleged "openness," official Soviet propaganda organs, including Pravda and Tass, began spreading the lie that the AIDS virus was created in a U.S. "germ warfare" experiment that went awry.[8] There is no possibility whatsoever that the Soviet leadership actually believes this; it is clearly a policy that asks, "Of all possible lies, which one will most discredit America with the Third World?" In the face of such actions, on what grounds could any rational person conclude that the Soviets genuinely seek better relations?

Finally, let us earnestly hope that we never become so weak and demoralized that the Soviets can conclude that the greatest blow to go unretaliated might be as large as a nuclear first strike!

Another faction seeking to strike the greatest blow that will remain unretaliated is made up of the various terrorist organizations striking at U.S. targets. As long as the argument "you can't fight back against terrorists, you must address the root causes of their grievances" prevails, terrorists will continue to have a wide zone of free attack to act against Americans in any way they please. But if capitalist achievement makes clear its intention to retaliate effectively against those states and/or organizations sponsoring or harboring terrorism—thereby reducing the size of the blow that will go unretaliated—the effectiveness of terrorism will decline dramatically.

In that part of the world where resentment prevails (and consequently economic development is virtually nil), a successful attack upon American and other Western interests is the greatest conveyor of status and prestige. This explains why the Soviets and their client states are so favorably regarded by "nonaligned" states that have made a policy of stifling economic development, even when they ought to rationally be perceived as an expansionist threat. We can reduce the international status conferred by America-bashing by refusing to submit meekly to such attacks and by refusing to subsidize resentful adversaries. When forced to choose between gratuitous displays of resentment and economic necessity, necessity will always win.

Doesn't such a policy carry the risk of a disastrous war with the Soviet Union? Quite the contrary; it reduces the danger of miscalculation considerably. The Soviets invariably respond with conciliation when the West displays relative firmess and resolve (as during Reagan's second term), and with expansionism in the face of Western pusillanimity (as under Ford and Carter). They enjoy delivering punches and jabs to Western interests, but they desperately need normal commercial relations with the West to carry along their moribund economy—a system derived from the resentments of life's failures that upholds as its highest principle that no one shall accumulate wealth through honest work. Were every attack upon our interests—whether verbal or physical-by-proxy (using Cubans, North Koreans, and so on)—resisted by a stiffened defense posture and appropriate commercial and financial sanctions, as well as by vigorous diplomatic and public-relations efforts, striking blows against the West would cease to be a profitable strategy. We must pursue the policy that experience shows will maximize the concessions made by our adversaries.

Our soft-headed thinkers are forever reminding us of the dangers we incur in attempting to defend ourselves. "Do not stand fast to any position," they urge, "even when it is the right one. We must not risk nuclear war." What they forget is that we are menaced by twin threats of mass extinction: nuclear war and extinction in resentment's death camps, which were so successful at exterminating "socially harmful" elements in the USSR that Hitler used them as a model for his own. Some things that decrease the likelihood of one calamity tend to increase the likelihood of the other. The solution is to find the course of action that minimizes the dangers of both. There is something more dangerous than displeasing the Soviets: pleasing them too well.

"The sole fate that the enemy (in the class war) deserves is annihlation": Soviet posters proclaimed this for years.[9] Remember that a proletarian state can only fully consolidate its power when the "bourgeois mentality" has been physically exterminated. Since that attitude describes the majority of Americans, we can expect that, at minimum, a hundred million deaths would be required for Soviet power to be consolidated here, even assuming a bloodless surrender. The only thing standing between many tens of millions of living Americans and a horrible, lingering death in a concentration camp in the frozen wilderness is our armed might. Solzhenitsyn refers to these camps as "Destructive Labor Camps," a point he illustrates profusely. This is reflected most clearly in the infamous dictate of Soviet prison labor boss Naftaly Aronovich Frenkel, one of the chief architects of the Gulag system: "The prisoner must be used up in the first three months." Many millions of those crushed in this holocaust were sentenced for nothing more substantial than falling under Article 7-35 of the Soviet Penal Code: "Socially Dangerous Elements."[10] (For some strange reason, although the Jewish Holocaust receives plenty of attention, it is unfashionable to lament the even greater number of victims slaughtered by the Bolsheviks. No doubt this is partly because, while it makes one feel virtuous to spit on the grave of a dead tyrant, few have the courage to face up to dictators who are still alive and very powerful.)

I personally am far more worried about dying in a concentration camp than about dying in a nuclear war, since recent global trends make the former far more probable. At least most of those who would perish in a nuclear war would die relatively quickly. They would not spend two months or more being tortured in interrogation. They would not spend an indeterminate amount of time being transported to "islands of the archipelago" in cattle cars, with many dying en route, and half of the rest perishing of starvation, exposure, and overwork every three months.

When seen in a broad historical perspective, the similarities between the present Soviet regime and the medieval Catholic Church are ominous, and they are too important to ignore. Both are possessors of a universal and Catholic doctrine that transcends all national and ethnic boundaries, outside of which there can be no salvation. Both have an Inquisition, which never rests; both allow absolutely no possibility of free discussion or dissent. Both have an Index of Forbidden Books, and censor all writings that deviate however slightly from their perception of absolute truth. Both ceaselessly seek out heretics—both real and imagined—and frequently torture them so severely that they freely confess to entering into all manner of bizarre pacts with the Enemy of Truth— confessions which seem utterly absurd to those outside the True Faith. Both support crusaders and conquistadores whose job is to spread the Gospel of Truth to foreign lands. If the natives in these lands refuse to accept the Truth, then they must be put to the sword, for this Truth is more important than life itself. Indiginous cultures are crushed, and the True Faith is established in their place. There is, however, one significant difference between the two: The medieval Catholic Church is recognized by all thinking people as one of the most abominable chapters in human history; but the Soviet regime is regarded as "progressive" by people who should be smart enough to know better.

Resentment is an implacable enemy of any culture that dares to encourage and accept earthly, material success. It is an enemy with which one cannot genuinely reason or negotiate, for it holds only revengefulness toward those whose success makes its own failure the more acutely painful, and it will stop at nothing to gain eventual victory over its enemy. Does this view sentence us to the inevitability of a new world war? Not at all. We can prevent global war if we can preserve achievement long enough for the privileged hierarchies in Marxist countries to lose their proletarian leanings and sympathies. Eventually, concessions must be made to induce achievement within the Soviet Union, and a new bourgeois society in which property and other human rights are respected will be created. Like an entirely Christian society, an entirely Marxist society is in open conflict with reality. For reasons of doctrine, it must be in perpetual war against achievement because the fruit of achievement is wealth, and wealth is equated with sin. Nonetheless, in order for that society to survive and remain to some degree competitive with the more humane and rational societies of the world, achievement must be encouraged. Thus, compromises must inevitably be made— a phenomenon already occurring in almost every Marxist country at this time.

Every society needs achievers to keep it productive and growing. No society can afford to make war upon achievement forever; to do so is to perish. In order to motivate achievers, however, great inequality must be tolerated, for differences in wealth between classes act like voltage differences that accelerate charged particles: They represent the differential that makes it possible for particles to break free and jump. When all are pressed down in a state of wretchedly equal poverty, there is no more possibility of extracting energy from achievers than from an electrically neutral conducting rod; for if no extraordinary reward accompanies extraordinary risk or effort—and especially if achievement is discouraged by the prevailing philosophy— achievement will be so minimal that the society may need outside assistance just to preserve everyone at subsistence levels. But when achievers can see others around them who have earned their earthly reward, they strive mightily to do likewise.

In a few centuries at most, perhaps much less, the newly privileged classes that rule the USSR will have distanced themselves so greatly from the revengeful rabble from which they arose that they will begin to perceive themselves as aristocrats. They are already acquiring a cultivated taste for the world's arts and luxuries, to which only they have access. They will perceive an ever-increasing gap between themselves and their chauffeurs and servants. They may even eventually become truthful, as they establish long-term relationships and alliances with other powerful persons. Resentment will be no more real to them than to the wealthy Christian, who only recites anti-wealth religious doctrines on ceremonial occasions. At such a time, fruitful discussions about peace and disarmament will indeed be possible. But by then they will not be needed.

After all, that old scourge the Roman Catholic Church is still with us, having over the centuries lost all its teeth. The same is true of many once rabidly fanatical Protestant denominations. While nominally clinging to the same doctrines, today these churches fall all over themselves to compromise with their enemies, often even conceding to them the moral "high ground." (For what is the so-called "liberation theology" if not a capitulation to the Church's powerful rival, Marxism?) If these churches today had even a tenth of the fanatical intolerance they once possessed, they would now be locked in a struggle to the death with their socialist rivals, instead of nodding in silent agreement as Marxists denounce wealth, standing in awe of *their* fanaticism. And if Christ's once-ferocious church can keep all of its external form and structure while remaining only a shadow of its brutal former self, I can see no reason that the church of Karl Marx cannot do the same.

The history of the world since the late eighteenth century seems to be nothing more than the various forms of resentment playing themselves out. All revolutions, with one major exception, swept into power with the promise to transform that nation into a paradise on earth; but instead of a paradise, the result was a hell of murderous violence. Whether socialist, fascist, or religious; whether in France, Russia, Germany, China, Iran, Cambodia, or Vietnam; when the previous regime was swept away by a violent uprising, the end was inevitably bloodshed and ruin. The only significant exception to this grim pattern was the American revolt against British rule. While it was not without some unnecessary domestic bloodshed, by and large the rebellion and its aftermath were as peaceful as a violent revolution could possibly be. What explains the enormous difference between the American Revolution and all the others?

The American Revolution was the only large-scale political revolution that was not fueled primarily by proletarian resentment. George Washington, Thomas Jefferson, John Adams, James Monroe, and the other revolutionary leaders can hardly be described as proletarian. The leaders of the American Revolution were some of the richest men in the United States. They were educated, self-restrained aristocratic gentlemen, thoroughly imbued with the upper-class values of honesty, fairness, justice, tolerance, and liberty. They sought to defend those values against a capricious and power-hungry sovereign. Thomas Jefferson and Benjamin Franklin, whose accomplishments outside the political arena are celebrated even today, were among the greatest achievers of the eighteenth century. Clearly, the leaders of the American Revolution were among the "truthful ones." Theirs was an aristocratic radicalism. They had absolutely nothing in common with the radicalism of the revengeful rabble, which has caused all subsequent political revolutions. When the American revolutionaries came to power, they harbored no resentments against wealth, for they were the wealthy. They did not nurse any long-standing grudges or vindictiveness. They sought to establish a government that would make it safe to be truthful.

Reflect on the significance of the first president, George Washington, and every subsequent president stepping down from the presidency when the law required it. They peacefully and trustingly handed over power, sometimes to a rival political party. What splendidly noble actions! Each leader graciously yielded his power, confident that the next president would be truthful enough to yield power in turn. This noble dance has continued without interruption for two centuries, through many major crises. No president or other leader of any party has ever failed to step down upon the expiration of his term of office or tried to prevent subsequent elections. Contrast this with the behavior of vermin like Hitler or Lenin, who participate in elections only as a charade,

ROBERT SHEAFFER

masking their true intentions as they prepare to savagely seize power, and having no intention of ever relinquishing it once successful. They are mendacious in the extreme.

Democracy only works well when the populace is, on the whole, truthful enough to participate in fair elections and demand that all candidates and election officials play by the rules, which includes giving up power when required to do so. Thus the population must generally share the noble attributes of fairness, tolerance, justice, respect for others' persons and property, and the willingness to subordinate illicit short-term gain to lasting principle. In countries in which the large majority shares the proletarian outlook, democracy cannot take root. To them, elections are to be won by intimidation and/or cheating (or else just one party is allowed to participate). Power, once taken, is never voluntarily relinquished. Such a country is not yet truthful enough to be a democracy. It is also not yet ready to generate affluence, which requires a lifetime of commitments honored.

For any significant economic growth to occur, truthfulness must first reach a critical mass. This has not yet occurred in many Third World countries, where theft-oriented proletarian values prevail. Because of the "de-colonialization" occurring in recent decades, resulting in the retreat of the former European colonial rulers, truthfulness has declined considerably in the governments of the former colonies, and plunder has increased in proportion. Native hooligans with theft-oriented values have seized the reins of state in nearly every former European colony, and they wield unlimited power until it is stolen by the next savage, who likewise has no intention of ever giving it up. This tends to defer economic growth indefinitely. The old European

169

colonial rulers were eventually persuaded to leave their former colonies peacefully, for isn't it only fair that these people should rule themselves? But one will never persuade Idi Amin, Muammar Qaddafi, Emperor Bokassa, or the Cuban soldiers in the Soviet Foreign Legion to behave as nobly.

Consequently, the nondemocratic nations seethe with resentment against the wealth and power of the democratic, industrialized Western alliance, shrieking that colonialism, racism, sexism, Zionism, imperialism, apartheid, and exploitation have "caused" their poverty. But poverty is not "caused" or created: it is the default condition of the human race, the absence of advanced economic development. Robinson Crusoe lived in extreme poverty. It is wealth that must be "caused," poverty being the name applied to its absence. Over the years, some nations have managed to generate considerable affluence by pursuing policies that allow achievers to keep and enjoy the fruits of their labors. Achievement-oriented policies lead to the investment of any wealth not immediately consumed into financial ventures that generate future wealth. But where resentment prevails, wealth exists to be plundered, achievement is severely discouraged, and investment for future prosperity becomes impossible. As long as wailing on the part of the plunderers inspires sympathy in the West and brings bribes in the form of "foreign assistance," we can expect to keep hearing this refrain. However, should we someday find the courage to truthfully reply that their failure to develop capitalist affluence is a consequence of their own shortcomings, and that we will in no way support or subsidize resentment against ourselves, the degree of venomous anti-Americanism in the world would decline dramatically.

170

ROBERT SHEAFFER

The greatest disaster that can befall any society is to be conquered by a movement fueled primarily by the resentments of that society's own worst elements. Such a disaster removes from power the finest, most self-disciplined achievers, whose rule is characterized by tolerance and respect for human rights, bringing into absolute power the most violently resentful. Not only does such a disaster inevitably bring great bloodshed and a drastic decline in living standards, in liberty, and in overall accomplishment, but if it persists long enough it can paralyze a society for centuries as the foundations of the very concepts of "good" and "bad" are changed from achievement-based to resentment-based. Thus, a "good" person is no longer thought of as one who accomplishes praiseworthy things in a framework of noble behavior, but as one who obeys authority unquestioningly and hates the "right" group: foreigners, or Jews, or infidels, or the wealthy. Such resentment-disasters befell the Roman civilization in the fourth century; France in 1789; Russia in 1917; Italy in 1922; Germany in 1932; China in 1949; Vietnam and Cambodia in 1975; and Nicaragua and Iran in 1979. (There were many others of lesser note.) In some cases, these revolutionary movements started out as pluralistic, but as soon as the forces of resentment were able to seize control, all pluralism and tolerance were crushed, for those are upper-class values, which are therefore alien to the angry proletariat.

A few nations and cultures have been fortunate enough to escape—either completely or nearly so—from being wrecked by the resentments of their own least productive citizens. The United States, Britain, Canada, and Australia have escaped nearly all recent effects; and these countries are consequently quite free

171

and prosperous, although they suffer from the lingering effects of ancient Christian and neo-Christian resentment and thus waste considerable resources bleeding their best achievers to gratify their worst. The same is true of much of Western Europe.

Japan has never suffered a proletarian disaster, and as an additional advantage has never been Christianized. Consequently, its people are hard-working and confident, and their fortunes are powerfully rising. They do not think themselves wicked when they succeed. Those Chinese in Hong Kong and Taiwan who have escaped the clutches of Mao Tse-Tung have also escaped all direct effect of the Chinese proletarian disaster, as have the people in Singapore, Indonesia, and other non-communist Asian countries. They may someday be as prosperous as the Japanese. (But even on Asia's Pacific rim, resentment is already rearing its ugly head. In Singapore, in Malaysia, and indeed throughout Southeast Asia, the affluence of the hard-working ethnic Chinese is generating profound resentment among less-productive native peoples. In Fiji, resentment against the wealth acquired by hard-working immigrants from India triggered a military coup in 1987 by Fijian natives, which resulted in the overthrow of the democratically elected government. Much of what is called "racism" today is nothing more than resentment against the achievements of ethnic groups who hold success-oriented values.)

Even the Jews, although they have been attacked many times and millions have been killed by resentful Christians and Moslems, have always faced an enemy on the outside. Today Jews in Israel and other democratic countries tend to be highly successful because of their strong work ethic. It seems that nations and cultures can in some circumstances survive and recover even from

172

ROBERT SHEAFFER

a devastating military defeat, and become once again prosperous and self-confident; but it takes hundreds—even thousands—of years to overcome the disaster of prolonged rule by derelicts from within.

NOTES

1. This hypothesis is expressed in Lenin's hilariously funny book *Imperialism, The Highest Stage of Capitalism* (New York: International Publishers, 1933), which would qualify as high comedy were its ultimate consequence not so tragic. Lenin vituperates with anger as he describes the rapid economic growth in Europe under capitalism, and in their colonies as well. Instead of welcoming this growth, he sees it as proof of sinister conspiracies. His depiction of the developed countries forcibly exporting their "surplus of capital" to poorer nations is humorous in the extreme; I cannot help but imagine a holdup-in-reverse, "Take my money or I'll take your life."

2. Solzhenitsyn, *The Gulag Archipelago* (New York: Harper & Row, 1973), part 1, chapter 2.

3. *The Gulag Archipelago,* part 3, chapter 10; part 4, chapter 4.

4. *The Gulag Archipelago,* part 3, chapter 3; see also part 3, chapter 11. Solzhenitsyn writes that with the coming of the Russian Revolution, "It was found both useful and amusing that they [thieves] were enemies of private property and therefore a revolutionary force which had to be guided into the mainstream of the proletariat, yes, and this would constitute no special difficulty."

5. *The Gulag Archipelago,* part 1, chapter 10 (engineers); part 1, chapter 8 (Lenin's remark).

6. *The Gulag Archipelago,* part 1, chapter 7 (preventive extermination); part 1, chapter 2 (individual nobility).

7. Revel, *How Democracies Perish* (New York: Doubleday, 1983), chapter 15. Ceausescu's remark was reported by a former top aide, now living in the United States; see Ion M. Pacepa, *Red Horizons: Chronicles*

of a Communist Spy Chief (Washington, D.C.: Regnery Gateway, 1987). L'affaire Daniloff: When the United States arrested Gennadi Zakharov in 1986, a Soviet spy who did not have diplomatic immunity, the Soviets promptly arrested Nicholas Daniloff, a reporter for *U.S. News and World Report,* on trumped-up spy charges, then offered to trade him for Zakharov. The Reagan administration, while pretending to be "tough" on hostage-takers, caved in to Soviet demands, trading the spy for the journalist.

8. See *OMNI,* July, 1987. This story has also been widely reported in the *Wall Street Journal,* and other places. On the "CBS Evening News," Dan Rather swallowed the Soviet fabrication without any apparent investigation, reporting the "Pentagon created AIDS" story as if it might be true; see "CBS News Suckered By The Soviets," by Reed Irvine, in *Human Events,* April 18, 1987. By 1988, the "Pentagon created AIDS" story had become an embarrassment to pretensions of *glasnost,* and was gradually abandoned. It was replaced by the yarn (*Tass,* January 9, 1988) that the U.S. was developing a "race weapon" to kill dark-skinned people, which it planned to give to South Africa.

9. *The Gulag Archipelago,* part 3, chapter 2.

10. *The Gulag Archipelago,* part 3, chapter 3 (both references). We also find a discussion of "socially dangerous elements" in *Totalitarianism* by Hannah Arendt (New York: Harcourt, Brace, & World, 1966).

8.
The Future

The two most significant developments of the last few centuries are the explosive growth in science and technology, and the slow, lingering death of religion. The two are not unrelated; indeed, the former is the primary cause of the latter. The principal reason for religion's long, slow decline is the dramatic increase in our knowledge of the universe, which we can clearly see to be following natural, not supernatural, laws.

A major contributing factor in religion's decline is a greater understanding of human psychology and of different human societies, each of which has its own tribal superstitions. Inevitably, we compare other tribal superstitions with our own. Every tribe, without exception, holds to its own aboriginal belief system with the utmost certainty, yet every belief system is mutually contradictory. Only the abysmally provincial can believe for long that the universe operates according to unfathomable, supernatural laws, and that their tribe alone has unique and metaphysically certain answers to those mysteries.

As knowledge continues to increase over time—as it surely will unless civilization itself is destroyed—the advances of natural science will leave less and less room for religious mysteries. For centuries, religion (and not only Christianity) has been colliding with known facts about the real world, and each year the impact of these collisions increases. With each collision, a tiny bit of the fabric of religion is worn away. This change is not visible on a year-by-year basis, but over the long term it results in a very serious erosion.

Do not object by saying that we are currently in the midst of a religious revival, although we surely are; for when seen in the long-term context, the current resurgence of religion is quite insignificant—a minor rally in a gigantic bear market. The path downward from every peak has many brief but steep rises, and if we sample the degree and influence of religion at fifty-year intervals, the trend shows an unbroken decline. A century ago Nietzsche wrote, "God is dead, but given the way of men, there may still be caves for thousands of years in which his shadow will be shown."[1]

As religion evaporates, it does not do so uniformly. The lighter parts evaporate the most quickly: guardian angels; crude peasant miracles; personal visitations from divine beings; relics, such as the Holy Foreskin and the milk of the Blessed Virgin (hence *Liebfraumilch*); and an ass that speaks in a human voice, berating its master for treating it so harshly.[2] The heavier parts remain longer: religious-based habits deeply ingrained into human thought and action, and especially the religion's concepts of virtue and of human nature. These may temporarily take on secular roots as their celestial foundations crumble—as Marx has now taken over enforcement of Christ's morality—but eventually even these attitudes will vanish unless reinforced by observation and experience.

But even neo-Christianity is now also in open conflict with reality. Each year the once-shining promises made by socialists of all stripes are seen to be increasingly mendacious, dirty, and threadbare. Nowhere has socialism liberated the mind; nowhere has it brought prosperity; and nowhere has it brought any kind of freedom whatsoever. Everywhere it has been tested it has brought only a shabby stagnation, and a degree of misfortune proportional to the degree of socialism inflicted on the people. Where its concentration has been relatively mild—in Western democracies—it has resulted in high taxation, declining living standards, and stagnation in once-robust economies. Where its victory has been complete, it has utterly abolished all civil liberties and resulted in an economy of chronic shortages, in which people wait in long lines to buy basic items of food and clothing.

Socialism, in all its forms, represents a value system grounded in the resentments of those who have failed in open economic competition. To redress these failures, it turns to that proletarian shortcut to wealth: theft. Its thirst for revenge against the formerly successful endures long after the victim's expropriation has been complete, long after they have ceased to be a credible threat. It leads to savage and inhuman violence. What socialism seeks to create is a government of the failures, by the failures, and for the failures, to establish an economy in which there is no penalty for being inert. However, the other side of that coin is that there is no reward for success, and in the absence of rewards, few will discipline and drive themselves to make material success possible. The result is a way of life so dismal that the desire to escape is widespread, but the state's guards at the border have orders to shoot to kill anyone who tries.

Marxist countries are very visible failures in an era of increasingly high technology. They are backward lands where math is still done on an abacus—while schoolchildren in capitalist countries wear wristwatches with built-in calculators, then come home to play with sophisticated computers in their own bedrooms. Those countries on Asia's Pacific rim that have turned their backs on socialism completely have in recent decades experienced explosive economic growth. Their neighbors who have fallen into the Marxist abyss remain mired in poverty and totalitarian oppression, hell-holes from which everyone who can escape, does. A dozen years after their "liberation" from capitalism, all socialism has brought to the people of Vietnam is widespread malnutrition, concentration camps, and the extermination of human freedom, while people in nearby free-market countries have both their liberty and a rapidly expanding prosperity. The case against socialism is now ironclad.

Each year, the clash of socialism with reality becomes greater. Over time (unfortunately, a very long time), socialism will become as eroded from its initial ferocity as today's tepid Christianity is from the fanatacism of Tertullian and Torquemada. This same erosion, due to the conflict between dogma and reality, is visible in the Soviet Union, China, and other Marxist countries even today. Unfortunately, it operates extremely slowly.

As technology advances, the proliferation of powerful personal computers and related information technology is creating unparalled opportunities for self-directed individual achievement. With the accumulation of capital investment in productive technology in all fields increasing the rewards of achievement, the sullen and resentful are increasingly being left behind in the dust. Each technological advance enables achievers to accomplish more per day than ever before, while those who sit back and do nothing will continue to reap exactly that: nothing, regardless of how much technology is, or is not, available. This both widens and accelerates the gap between the "knows" and the "know nots," the "do's" and the "do not's"; (for people conveniently forget that those "have nots" so pitied and honored in resentment's litany are typically not only "have nots," but they are also "do nots," "can nots," "will nots," and nearly always "think nots" as well).

As achievers quicken their pace, assisted by marvelous future inventions that today are not yet even conceived, those who sit and wallow in resentment will be left farther and farther behind. Inevitably, a tremendous roar will go up, hollering that the rapid progress of technology must stop, and that the resentful must be respectfully carried along on achievers' shoulders. When we hear this ferocious roaring, we must not bow down before it as if it were a lofty moral statement, for it is mere flatulence. Let us instead greet it with contempt and even dare to laugh courageous laughter, taunting those roaring with rage to get up out of the mud and try to run alongside us. If they try to, but stumble, let us compassionately *hold out our hand* to catch them and help them try to become runners like us. But should they curse us for our speed as we run by, let us give them no further thought, leaving them to fend for themselves without our hand-outs. They will tire of that very soon. No longer getting free lunches through the misplaced pity of achievers, they will be forced to stop playing their old games and learn to become at least minimal achievers. Some of them will surprise even them-selves when they see what can be accomplished in just a few years!

A society is healthy when its morality recognizes and en-courages its achievers, permitting them to keep the fruits of their own labors, unplundered by the envious hordes. In such a situation, commerce, science, and the arts flourish; and future historians will lavish praise upon that splendid civilization. Even the finest societies, however, have many people who are failures, for reasons intrinsic to themselves. Of course they will blame everyone but themselves for their problems, for such is human nature. However, only in decadent societies is the whining of the inept mistaken for a lofty moral statement. Should a society's achievers begin to identify more strongly with the complaints of these losers than with the accomplishments of people like themselves, they will become paralyzed by guilt, and the future will look bleak.

One of the most visible signs of decadence is when many people in the middle ranges of society begin to take their ideals and their values from the classes below them—from the angry and the unproductive—rather than from the classes above, who for the most part got where they are by accomplishing something worthwhile. It has now become fashionable for middle-class youth to dress and act like slum dwellers rather than trying to emulate the educated and self-disciplined classes. Clearly, slum rock has achieved an almost total victory over all other contemporary musical expressions. At what other point in history has the music and the accompanying culture of the very bottom class been the *de facto* standard for popular entertainment? Nonconfrontational popular music was the norm until very recently, but today jazz and folk music are dying, and pre-rock popular music is all but dead. Even Walt Disney productions, which once provided spectacles of innocence and glee for children, has now capitulated, merging slum rock into its movies and cartoons. (And we now have widespread nostalgia for an allegedly "simpler" time; what we actually yearn for is a vanished, far more civilized era when the average person derived his ideals from the gentler classes above him, not from the revengeful mob below.)

As an example of decadence, consider how the French aristocracy was delighted by Rousseau's fashionably crude primitivism in the decades before that foppish aristocracy failed to effectively oppose an uprising by the revengeful proletariat, which sent many of them to the Guillotine. Because civilization is nothing more than the sum total of all its achievements, when resentment becomes fashionable in respectable circles, it suggests that an era of achievement—and consequently a chapter of civilization—may be coming to an end.

Those who are only partly given over to resentment hold that while modest economic success is allowable—even virtuous— at some point the pursuit of honest profit becomes sinful, especially when its success becomes too great. Of course, nobody has ever been able to clearly delineate this point, or to give us reasonably

181

plausible guidlines for recognizing it, or to explain how and why virtuous activity can insensibly merge into sin. The embarrassing answer is that affluence becomes "sinful" when it is large enough and conspicuous enough to generate resentment; and the reason this transition cannot be identified clearly is that the threshold of resentment varies with each individual.

Most middle-class Americans feel only twinges of resentment here and there. They are perfectly willing to allow small or midsized businesses their profits, but there is usually some threshold of size above which a major corporation is felt to be "too big"; in which case the government needs to "do something" about it. Typically, giant corporations such as IBM, Exxon, or AT&T fall into this category of imagined wickedness, not from any specific wrongdoing that they are alleged to have committed but from uncontrollable envy over these companies' "excess profits." The executives of such corporations know how much discipline was required to earn those profits, and as they look at their rising costs and stiff competition they wonder how much profit might be left for making the investments that will be critical for their future success, after paying confiscatory business taxes of 50 percent or more. The slum dweller who burns with resentment against anyone who is not a failure like himself would not only eagerly plunder the profits of businesses large and small if given a chance (as illustrated by the wide-spread looting that occurs whenever there is a city-wide power outage), but also considers the pocket cash of the typical middle-class American to be fair game. He concocts hustles and scams galore to try to tap into this wealth; and not infrequently takes more direct action, slugging almost anyone over the head when the opportunity to steal a purse or a wallet presents itself. Thus, the suitability of a target for plunder is in the eyes of the beholder.

Resentment-morality teaches, "Blessed are the poor, for it is they alone who are truly good." But if these people are so good, why do they remain poor? Certainly, among the principal virtues in any civilized society are dependability, thrift, careful planning, and a respect for the person and property of others. Such virtues are conspicuously absent in proletarian culture today. Why should one be called good when one displays none of these virtues? I think it is more appropriate to say, "Blessed are those who can accomplish something worthwhile."

Resentment-morality teaches, "Blessed are the weak, for they shall enter the kingdom of heaven." It is no disgrace if one must be weak, but it is better to try to be strong. Some are weak in body, and cannot do anything to grow stronger. Others are strong in body but resentful in their thinking, and they seek only to bring down anything that is successful. All they can achieve is destruction.

Resentment-morality teaches, "Blessed are those who take the default option in life." But it is better to strive to achieve *something* than to sit back and wallow in misery; for negative entropy is a virtue. A cow can easily practice the Christian virtues of passivity and resignation. However, it takes a competent human being to strive for—and achieve—a worthwhile goal. (Indeed, Gibbon makes a strong case for believing that the Roman emperor Constantine may have made Christianity the religion of his empire not out of genuine personal conviction, but from a desire to render his subjects passive and obedient.[3] That it might also render them indigent and intolerant seems not to have occurred to him.)

Resentment-morality preaches self-denial and resignation, in direct opposition to life's instincts. But the achiever practices self-discipline in order to further his own interests and better satisfy life's instincts. There are many circumstances in which both will practice restraint, although for different reasons. This confuses many people. They assume that if life's instincts were not throttled, then everyone would charge about uncontrollably, as they would. They do not understand that only for those lacking effective self-restraint does this crushing of the instincts become necessary. When external discipline must be applied, it is extremely difficult to gauge the exact dose required, much like the problem facing diabetics whose bodies cannot manufacture insulin, and who must therefore inject it from an outside source. The dose is often somewhat too large or too small, with serious consequences attending excesses in either direction.

Resentment-morality teaches, "Blessed are the credulous, for they accept religious claims without asking to see proof." But credulity is *never* a virtue.

Summing up all its highest principles, resentment-morality proclaims, "Blessed are those who have made a mess of their lives." But any society that truly believes that it is blessed to fail will not long prevail on this earth.

All parents wish good things for their children and want them to grow up to be moral adults. Resentment-morality would dictate that proper parents should instruct their children to grow up to be lazy, indigent, profligate, and ignorant—in short, to be economic failures—in order that they may be among the truly good, the wretched. In actuality, of course, parents strive for precisely the opposite, although they don't always accomplish it: They seek to prepare their children to earn at least a moderately good living. But to be consistent with their professed ideals, parents who are sincere Christians or socialists should prepare their children for a lifetime of poverty and begging, and impress upon them the virtue of being unemployed, so that the children may someday become disgusting enough to be counted among the truly good.

It is noble to feel great sympathy for the truly helpless: the very young, the very old, the very sick, and the infirm. These people are weak, and not as a consequence of a lifetime of making bad choices. (Note that I am not including lazy or unproductive adults among the truly helpless.) It is profoundly noble to help them, not out of a sense of guilt or obligation but as an affirmation of one's own fundamental goodness and strength; for one of the ways that goodness manifests itself is in freely showering benefits upon anyone it deems worthy of such largesse, with no expectation of any direct benefits in return. The achiever is motivated by a sense of abundant, overflowing life, and his sense of power and competence is enhanced by his own ability to change things in a positive way. The greater the scope of one's achievements, the greater one's potential benificence.

Throughout recorded human history, the ebb and flow of the love of achievement—and the resentment against its success—have been major forces behind the rise and fall of civilizations and empires. A civilization thrives as long as achievement-oriented values are cherished by the citizenry at large, and especially by its middle and upper classes. As soon as the morality of resentment gains the upper hand, that which holds the civilization together loses credibility and moral force, and it ultimately perishes. When something is taxed, you get less of it; and when something is subsidized, you get more of it. Presently, we place a heavy tax on achievement but subsidize the resentful, who reject the need for learning and the discipline of work. This causes a decrease in achievement and an increase in resentment, in proportion to the size of the income transfer. It is not difficult to see how to diminish resentment to very low levels: Simply stop giving free lunches to angry failures. Not only will this provide an enormous boost to achievers by allowing them to keep nearly all the fruits of their accomplishments, but the resentful, forced to make the difficult adjustment to actually earn their own keep, will soon discover that even they can be surprisingly successful when they put a little effort into it.

Resentment thrives on the pusillanimity of those oriented toward achievement, on their acceptance of excuses, and on their willingness to take onto themselves the burden and responsibility for others' failures. Those weighted down with "liberal guilt" are, after all, playing the role expected of good Christians: diligently shouldering that religion's yoke of unearned guilt and sin. The proletariat is far too undisciplined to succeed at Christian submission (or much of anything else); failing to renounce their desire for worldly goods, they blame their economic problems on someone else, and demand solutions. And then achievers, tireless strivers that they are, try to solve their problems for them. This leaves the superior pack-animal in the position of carrying two peoples' loads of guilt, as well as the worldly toil of both.

As long as guilt-ridden achievers are moved by excuses offered for chronic economic failure, resentment will continue to be a profitable strategy. The resentful are ceaselessly generating new excuses and mutating old ones, a Darwinian process which leads to the survival and proliferation of the fittest excuses for extracting sympathy from achievers. However, resentment can be all but eliminated (or more correctly, sent into long-term remission) should achievement find the courage to re-acknowledge and strongly reaffirm its own values. To the resentful, achievers must say in one united voice: "I am tired of listening to your excuses. You are undisciplined and unproductive. That is a full and complete explanation of your poverty. You, the poor, are not the blessed or the good; those terms apply to the people who have been paying your bills all these years. You are a failure, and your behavior needs to change. I will not support you any longer. You must accept whatever employment is available to you, even if you do not like it. If you become violent, we will lock you up for a very long time, and if you kill anyone, we will kill you. After you have disciplined yourself to successfully hold down a job, even at the lowest level, you might want to think about getting more education, if you would like to eventually get a better job."

The achiever must strive to free himself from harboring or identifying with any form of resentment manifested against any form of success; for not only is the expression of resentment a sign of the abysmally bad judgment and failure-prone attitude that suggest a petty and vindictive nature, but to harbor resentment limits one by turning one toward destructiveness instead of toward accomplishment. Envy is self-punishing.

We must recapture the courage and confidence of the thinkers of the Enlightenment, as well as their liberation from resentment-derived Christian values. Most people do not realize the degree to which the eighteenth-century philosophers rejected not only Christian theology but many of its moral teachings as well, preferring to identify with proud, tolerant, aristocratic, pagan thinkers like Cicero, Epicurus, and Lucretius. We sometimes think of the philosophes as timid religious skeptics—which some of their writings might suggest, if we forget the obstacles they faced. All books had to be approved by government censors, and the threat of prison for heresy was very real: Diderot and Voltaire actually spent time in prison, and others escaped the same fate only by quickly slipping across international borders. The philosophes' private writings plainly show the depth of their contempt for Christian values.

Peter Gay, a noted historian of the Enlightenment, has summarized the Enlightenment's view of the origin of Christianity as follows: "Late in the first century of our era, an insidious force began to insinuate itself into the mentality of the Roman Empire. Slyly exploiting men's fears and anxieties and offering grandiose promises of eternal salvation, Christianity gradually subverted the self-reliant paganism that had sustained the ruling class. . . . In its early history, in its very origins, there was something unsavory about Christianity. Significantly, it flourished in an age of decadence and among the lower orders, among men and women sunk in ignorance, vice and despair."[4]

Such was the consensus of the eighteenth-century philosophes, who obviously did not stand in awe of proletarian failures, as did many who came after them. Voltaire and Gibbon make frequent reference to the unreliability and apparent untruthfulness of the early Christian evangelists. When Diderot saluted Voltaire as "my sublime, honorable, and dear Anti-Christ," he was *flatter-*

ing Voltaire, not defaming him. (Not until a century later do we again encounter this same revulsion toward all things Christian, and this same identification with pagan authors, in the writings of the nineteenth-century German Anti-Christ. However, by then the world had changed so much that it did not even recognize the rebirth of Enlightenment values when it saw them.) "Every sensible man," wrote Voltaire, "every honorable man, must hold the Christian sect in horror." David Hume privately worried that the English were "relapsing fast into the deepest Stupidity, Christianity, & Ignorance."⁵ The age of the Enlightenment did not look kindly upon the Christian values of passivity, intolerance, ignorance, and failure, at least not until a man named Rousseau became a great celebrity by proclaiming civilization to be a curse. Nearly two centuries of irrationality, of religious revival, of powerful resurgence in nationalist and racialist thinking, was to follow.

The great Counter-Enlightenment has gone on long enough: a time of ascendant mysticism, of religious revival, of national "self-determination" and racial "awareness," and above all, the romanticization of proletarian values and the exaltation of failure and resentment as the highest ideals. We must find the courage to rescue the heritage of the Enlightenment from the disaster that overcame it when it failed to defend its vision of reason and liberty against violent lower-class resentments, which were finally able to burst forth in the anarchy of the French Revolution—that tragic episode in which the proletariat first tasted blood. Reason and liberty were unfairly blamed for resentment's crimes and became wrongly associated with anarchy and mass murder.

We must make it understood that a love of truthfulness and reason, manifested in an aristocratic radicalism, leads to a free, tolerant, and orderly state, a society in which everyone is safe. The fruits of achievement are protected, and the poor learn to become achievers both from necessity as well as from fashion. The radicalism of aristocratic gentlemen like George Washington, Thomas Jefferson, or George Mason leads to liberty; while the intolerant, lower-class, xenophobic radicalism of the likes of Robespierre or St. Paul, Lenin or Mussolini, Hitler or Mao Tse-Tung leads only to tyranny, suffering, and servitude.

Western civilization has suffered the supreme disaster once already—during the fourth and fifth centuries A.D.—when it was weakened and then conquered by a movement representing the intolerant and violent resentments simmering among the detritus in its own slums. The damage done to learning, to art, to civilization itself, was incalculable. It took a full thousand years for a robust recovery to get underway, and even today the residual effects of that disaster are still causing untold misery. We must not under any circumstances allow this to occur again.

Why should *any* people or government sink so low as to become a "proletarian state?" Why should not every state be governed by its finest achievers instead of its angriest failures?

"Proletarian, Thou Hast Conquered?" Only if the men and women of ability sit by as if paralyzed and allow it to happen, having been taught that the resentments of the nonachiever represent the voice of a higher morality. The "class war" being waged against you is real. Fight back. If "we truthful ones" cannot make our values prevail, brutal and mendacious values will rule in their place.

What does the future hold? That depends on whether resentment or achievement prevails as the dominant moral vision.

ROBERT SHEAFFER

NOTES

1. The phrase "God is Dead" occurs in several places in Nietzsche's writings. What he apparently meant by it was that traditional religion had lost its power to influence serious thinkers. Nietzsche's Zarathustra explains that God became so choked up with pity for the human race that He choked to death. The passage quoted is from *The Gay Science,* translated by Walter Kaufmann (New York: Vintage Books, 1974), book three, aphorism 108.

2. The talking ass is found in Numbers 22:21-30.

3. Gibbon, *The Decline and Fall of the Roman Empire,* chapter 20. For a number of years, the emperor Constantine was living like a practicing pagan but talking like a Christian. Gibbon accuses Constantine of "solemn and deliberate perjury" in concocting the famous story about seeing a cross in the sky before a battle, and suggests what the emperor's actual motive may have been for feigning a belief in Christianity.

4. Gay, Peter, *The Enlightenment: An Interpretation. The Rise of Modern Paganism* (New York: Alfred A. Knopf, 1966), chapter 4.

5. Diderot, Voltaire, and Hume are quoted in Gay, *The Rise of Modern Paganism,* chapter 7. An understanding of the Enlightenment as "modern paganism" is critical to the point I am trying to illustrate.

Index

Compiled by Charlene Sheaffer

INDEX

artists, 14, 97, 128, 132

arts, 55, 68, 80, 112‑113, 117, 124, 180

~politics in, 133

Axelrod, Robert, *The Evolution of Economic Cooperation,* 40, 41

bad, 93

Beethoven, Ludwig van, 125, 126

Bellamy, Edward, 79

blacks, 83

bourgeoisie, 42, 45, 55, 78, 121, 126, 129, 133, 158, 163

~in Russia, 151–152

Burke, Edmund, 27

~*Reflections on the Revolution in France,* 27

Calvinist outlook, 81

Cambodia, 34, 107, 148, 155

capitalism, 54, 79, 87, 106, 113, 130, 138, 145, 146, 148, 150, 154, 170, 178

Catholic Church, 166

~medieval, 164

chemicals, 105

Chernobyl, 103

children, 12, 13, 14, 49, 59, 61, 67, 68, 178, 184

China, 18, 148, 155, 172, 178

Christianity, 17, 18, 19, 20, 23, 35, 45, 77, 78, 79, 81, 83, 85, 91, 92, 106, 107, 165, 166, 172, 176, 177, 178, 183, 185, 186, 188

civilization, 8, 9, 10, 11, 15, 56, 59, 72‑73, 83, 91, 96, 97, 124, 127, 144, 176, 180, 185, 190

~ancient, 16

~Chinese, 19

~definition, 8, 99–100

~human race corrupted by, 98, 189

~resentment against, 120, 123

class struggle, 12, 45, 141, 154, 155, 163, 190

~rock music as expression of, 124

communism, 34, 56, 148, 156

consciousness-raising, 87

Constantine, Emperor, 17, 183, 191

corporations, 182

dance, 119-120

Darwinism, 96, 101

democracy, 138, 143, 149, 159, 169

~socialism in, 177

Democratic party, 138, 140, 142

Diderot, Denis, 14, 98, 188

Donatist sect, 17

economic growth, 8, 9, 19, 24, 45, 100, 104, 105, 133, 169, 178

~as sin against nature, 100

~resentment against, 102, 103

economic order, spontaneous, 40

economy (of a nation), 12, 16, 90, 147

~Roman, 18

education, 55, 59–73, 187

~major functions, 69

~science, 114

Emerson, Ralph Waldo, 125

INDEX

Enlightenment, Age of, 19, 27, 28, 187, 189

environmental movement, 101
—and politics of resentment, 102

envy, 8, 10, 15, 24, 28, 52, 53, 67, 79, 81, 85, 92, 144, 159, 187

equality, 8

faith healing, 108, 109

fascism, 21, 22, 83, 88, 130–131, 139, 147

French Revolution, 26–27, 125, 189

fundamentalism (religious), 107, 140
—Islamic, 137, 140, 153

games theory, 40

genetic engineering, 104

Gibbon, Edward, 16, 17, 183, 188

good, 34, 93

Gorky, Maxim, 154

guilt, 10, 11, 12, 45, 51, 79, 87, 89, 91, 93, 180, 185, 186

happiness, 76, 77, 78, 81, 92

Henry VIII, 27

Hispanics, 83

Hitler, Adolph, 83–84, 131, 149, 157, 162, 168

honesty, 35, 37, 40, 42, 43, 45, 61

hostages, 150–151, 153, 156, 157

housing, 100–101

Hugo, Victor, 38
—*Les Miserables,* 38

humanities, 112–113

Hume, David, 98, 189

income redistribution, 141

Indians, American, 98–99

industrial revolution, 19

inequality, human, 126, 127

intellectuals, 53, 54, 55, 138, 148, 149, 154

Japanese (people), 22–23, 83
—Japan, 172

Jefferson, Thomas, 36, 167

Jews, 22, 83, 84, 130, 157, 163, 171, 172
—anti-Semitism, 130, 138, 147

Julian the Apostate, 16

Ku Klux Klan (KKK), 21, 138

labor unions, 54

law enforcement, 143–144

Lenin, V. I., 16, 146, 148, 152, 153, 154, 156, 168

Lewis, Oscar, *The Children of San-chez, La Vida,* 44

Lewis, Sinclair, 79

liberals, 27, 28, 84, 137

liberation, 90, 178
—theology, 167

libertarians, 138, 139, 140

liberty, 16, 79, 80, 81, 137, 143, 171, 177, 189
—of animals, 99

lower clases, 10, 13, 15, 16, 22, 23, 28, 35, 43, 49, 56, 57, 60, 61, 62, 68, 77, 90, 110, 124, 190
—culture, 127
—men, 68

luck, 69, 111, 115

INDEX

INDEX

—against nuclear power, 103
—against science, 96, 113
—as a virtue, 75, 76
—as political base, 139, 143
—in art, 133
—manifestations, 11, 15
—of frustrated ambition, 53
—roots of, 12
—social disguises, 12
ressentiment, 14
revolution, 16, 29, 129-130, 171 (see also American Revolution; French Revolution)
rock music, 38, 119, 120, 121, 123, 132, 181
Roman Empire, 16, 17, 23, 106, 188
romanticism, 98, 100
Rousseau, Jean-Jacques, 98, 181, 189
Russell, Bertrand, 79
St. Augustine, *City of God,* 17
St. Paul, 16
schools, 60, 62, 64, 65, 67, 72, 114
—private, 65-66
science, 95-116, 175-176, 180
Shakespeare, William, 122, 127
Shaw, George Bernard, 79, 130
Silicon Valley, 81, 105
Skeptical Inquirer, 109
Snow, C. P., 112
social classes, 33, 47, 48, 70
social justice, 12
socialism, 19, 21, 23, 36, 38, 52, 56, 76, 78, 79-80, 85, 92, 93, 107,

138-140, 142, 146, 152, 154, 177, 178
socialists, 129, 130, 185
Solzhenitsyn, Alexander, 151-152, 154, 155, 163
—*Gulag Archipelago,* 151, 152
Soviet Union, 33, 146, 148, 150-152, 156, 157, 160, 161, 162, 163, 164, 166, 178
taxation, 177, 186
—definition, 140
technology, 95, 104, 106, 107, 175, 178, 179
—and ecology, 100, 102
terrorism, 150, 161
Thoreau, Henry, 98
Three Mile Island, 103
treaties, with Soviets, 146, 158
truthfulness, 39, 41, 43, 166, 168, 169, 189
"truthful ones," 34, 35, 39, 41, 42, 56, 68, 72, 168, 190
United States, 138, 157, 159, 160, 161, 171
universities, 53, 71, 84, 86, 87
upper classes, 8, 9, 14, 15, 28, 48, 49, 60, 65, 68, 69, 73, 124, 127, 159, 185
—British, 41
—values, 42, 168, 171
urban bohemian, 51
utopia, 79
Vandals, 18

197

INDEX

About the Author

Robert Sheaffer was born in Chicago, Illinois, and received a bachelor's degree in mathematics and a master's degree in teaching from Northwestern University. His first book, a highly skeptical analysis of UFO mania entitled *the UFO Verdict: Examining the Evidence* (about which *Sky and Telescope* magazine said, "If you're only going to have one book on UFOs, this is the one"), was published by Prometheus Books in 1980. His writings and reviews have appeared in such diverse publications as *Omni,* the *Humanist, Reason, Spaceflight,* and *Astronomy,* and he is a regular contributor to the *Skeptical Inquirer.* Mr. Sheaffer lives in the San Francisco Bay area, where he has been working in software development for the computer industry since 1973.